Life Without End

A Reassuring Look at Life, Death and Beyond

Bob Hendren

D1522843

JOURNEY BOOKS

An SPC Publication
Austin, Texas 78765

A complete *Teacher Resource Kit* for use with
this paperback is available from your religious bookstore or
the publisher.

LIFE WITHOUT END
Copyright © 1981 by Sweet Publishing Company,
Box 4055, Austin, Texas 78765

All scripture quotations followed by an asterisk (*)
are Hendren's own translation from the Greek text.

Unless otherwise indicated, scripture quotations are from the
Revised Standard Version of the Bible, copyrighted in 1946,
1952, and 1971 by the Division of Christian Education,
National Council of Churches, and used by permission.

Edited by Ron Durham
Cover designed by Tom Williams

Printed in the U.S.A.
Library of Congress Catalog Card Number 80-54164
ISBN 0-8344-0118-5

Contents

Bob Hendren wishes for his family — his wife Joyce, his two daughters Debbie and Diane, and his son Bobby — a future that is secure in Christ.

1 Joy Now & Forever

The future—is history moving toward a definite goal, or is it anybody's guess? New waves of pessimism sweeping over the world today would suggest it's all downhill from here. Were Charles Dickens living today, and partaking of this gloomy spirit, he would write, "It was the worst of times," and leave out the part about "it was the best of times." Futurist groups contest with each other to pick the direst fate for mankind. Fatalistic social analysts see only frustration or starvation ahead. Science-fiction authors put man into Orwell's *1984* where he is deprived of all humanity. Behaviorists want to subject us to a group of controllers who would bring about a future with neither freedom nor dignity. In the face of this psychic onslaught many people sink deeper into apathy, knowing only that they live in a world running out of everything but problems.

Does the Bible Have an Answer?

What does the Bible say to such saddened, pessimistic people? It says we can live joyfully—even

5

in view of the end. But a serious communication problem exists right at this point. People are not getting the message of joy, for many who publicly air their views about the Bible and the future are themselves doggedly pessimistic. Their statements indicate they see the Bible only as a tour guide to doomsday. Jesus Christ is not presented as the source of present and future joy. Rather a morbid attention to world events is paramount. Every petty dictator becomes a potential Antichrist. Every innocent trade association looks like another Roman Empire. Every skirmish in the Middle East seems to threaten Armaggedon. Today's news becomes tomorrow's sermons. Precious little joy comes out of this all-too-pervasive viewpoint. Such views detract from the Bible's affirmation of a guaranteed future in Christ.

Lord of the Present Future

This book will point to the way the Bible treats the future. The center will be the Christ of the present and future, rather than sacred fortune-telling. The Bible can present the most hopeful message about the future, but only if its true center, Jesus Christ, is maintained.

This book also takes the position that the biblical teaching on the nature of the last things (eschatology) is designed to create and develop certain attitudes and behavior. To return to these emphases will certainly rescue this great message of joyous hope from the curious speculations which so abound in our time. The purpose of this book is that Christians may once again deal with the anxieties in their lives by reflecting that "the Lord is near" (Phil. 4:5).

The Key to Joy

One more book about the end of the world may provoke an "Oh, yeah?" from jaded victims of irresponsible predictions. "What sort of doomsday stuff are you peddling?" will be the ho-hum response of those burned by books purporting to deal with the future. No wonder people are turned off. The end result of all this eccentric exegesis has been to erode confidence in the Bible and to rob Christians of joy.

But this book is not primarily about the end, but about Christ. He is the key to joyful living in the present and to confident hope in the future. Jesus Christ counters fear of the future, created by religious systems which pose as exclusive interpreters of doomsday. Christ is given a subordinate role in such schemes. He is not presented as the great Redeemer-Savior, but at best as a sort of divine Emcee of future events. A book like the best-selling *The Late Great Planet Earth* is representative of this school of religion. By choosing eschatological fervor over the simple presentation of Christ, such systems distort the major emphasis of Scripture.

Eschatological Fervor

Anyone can be gripped by eschatological fervor, a burning desire to unravel the mysteries of the future. In an uncertain world such attempts gain rapid attention. People are so hungry for some word of hope, any word at all, that they will buy and believe anything.

Even the apostles of Christ had such an experience. They were in the grip of eschatological fervor, but Jesus swiftly redirected it toward more

important tasks. Shortly before Jesus' ascension to
God they asked him, "Will you at this time restore
the kingdom to Israel?" (Acts 1:6). Surely, after all
the kingdom parables of Jesus they should have
known that his kingdom was not political (John
18:36). But victims of eschatological fervor seldom
think of reality. Jesus' sharp re-orientation should
serve to bring such victims back to what is central:

> It is not for you to know times or seasons
> which the Father has fixed by his own au-
> thority. But you shall receive power when the
> Holy Spirit has come upon you; and you shall
> be my witnesses in Jerusalem, and in all Ju-
> dea and Samaria and to the end of the earth.
>
> Acts 1:7-8

Presenting the good news about Jesus—not specu-
lating about the end of the world—is what brings
joy to the world.

Jesus Stressed Joyous Hope

You cannot be robbed of joy, now or in the future, if you lean on Christ. Jesus put his major
stress not on speculation but on a joyous hope that
transforms both present and future: "These things
I have spoken to you, that my joy may be in you,
and that your joy may be full" (John 15:11). What
things had Jesus spoken? Why, everything in his
discourse found in John 13–16. The subject matter
ranges from the here to the hereafter, and Jesus
says all of it is designed to produce a joy which the
world does not share. The keynote is joy, which is
why Jesus says, "No one will take your joy from
you" (John 16:22).

How would this joy continue? Only by the reality behind Jesus' statement in 16:22, "I will see you again." This reference is primarily to his resurrection appearances and also to his continued presence with them in the Holy Spirit (John 14:15-17). Joy in the present is based on continuing to have Christ, now and forever! This emphasis is certainly truer to the Bible than finding the latest key to some celestial calendar. Jesus' presence among us now is a stronger guarantee of future well-being than any interpretive system. His presence goes to the root of our fears and confusion in a healing way. Christ's joy brings certainty because it is based on his competence and compassion.

Christ's Competence

The true starting point for future and present joy is the competence of Christ to accomplish our salvation. The eternal validity of his salvation is the source of all hope. We know he is able to deliver on our greatest need—salvation. This solid, present reality transforms our life now and brightens our future. This is the point of emphasis in a famous passage from Hebrews:

> The former priests were many in number, because they were prevented by death from continuing in office; but he holds his priesthood permanently, because he continues for ever. Consequently he is able for all time to save those who draw near to God through him, since he always lives to make intercession for them.

> Hebrews 7:23-25

If Christ can deliver in the present, he can certainly deliver in the future. Hans Kueng, the German scholar, has a comment which makes the point perfectly: "It is by hope itself that the present world and society are to be not only interpreted but changed."[1] The power of Christ rescues our present and assures our future. The competence of Christ for salvation alters our perspective and places one great "known" fact into our future—*We are his*.

Christ's Compassion

Another great fact emerges from the Bible to further increase our confidence in the future of the believer—the compassion of Christ. God's love in Christ is a continuing present assurance of a future worth having, for it will be a future of love. God does not give up on relationships: "I am sure that he who began a good work in you will bring it to completion at the day of Jesus Christ" (Phil. 1:6).

God's plans for us in Christ do not alter with time. Nothing in the history of religious speculation can give more comfort than this single passage from Hebrews:

> For he has said, "I will never fail you nor forsake you." Hence we can confidently say,
> "The Lord is my helper,
> I will not be afraid;
> what can man do to me?"
>
> Hebrews 13:5-6

Christ will remain close to us. He will not move. This is why the Hebrew writer goes on to say: "Jesus Christ is the same yesterday and today and for ever" (13:8). Christ's compassion does not falter. It is there in the present and future. Joy like this is good in all ages. It delivers us from future fear and future confusion.

Future Fear

If we abandon Christ as Lord of the here and now as well as Lord of the future, we deliver ourselves over to future fear. Speculative books on the future cannot deliver us from this fear; only Christ can. Sometimes in fearing the future people will choose to concentrate all their attention on the here and now. This can lead to several serious, joy-defeating attitudes. One of these has been called *carpe diem* or "live for today." The Roman poet Catullus expressed it this way:

> Lesbia, let's live and love
> without one thought for gossip of
> the boys grown old and stern.
> Suns go down and can return,
> but, once put out our own brief light,
> we sleep through one eternal night.[2]

A life-style wholly dedicated to the here and now is the result of this thinking. As the football coach who refused to invest in young players and build for the future said, "The future is now." Of course in a few years his team had all old players and no future or present. The present alone is not enough.

Strangely enough, even some believers react strongly against a future emphasis. The cause is easily traced. An enormous preoccupation existed in earlier days with "going to heaven." This emphasis often wiped out any meaningful concerns about the present. The misery of day-to-day existence became a religious commonplace. Songs reflected this viewpoint: "Here I labor and toil..."; "When life's weary road I tread..." Present misery and a decidedly materialistic view of the hereafter turned many believers to a complete preoccupation with the future.

The negative reaction of many people to such "pie-in-the-sky" ideas is understandable. Blessings of the present life were often completely overlooked, although the Bible has much to say about present blessings. The future is seen, biblically, as that period when present blessings reach their ultimate level. But we do not have to make a choice between having a present or having a future. In Christ we can have both!

Possessing the Present and Future

In Christ we have the best of both worlds, present and future. The secular person does not have to "live it up" at the expense of his future. Nor does the believer have to accept a concept of present misery to enjoy a glorious future. In Christ we can have it all. Christ bridges the gap between present and future. The Bible declares this quite strongly:

> So then, let no one take pride in men; for all things are yours, whether Paul, whether Apollos, whether Cephas, whether the world, whether life, whether death, whether the present, whether the future, all belong to you, and you belong to Christ, and Christ to God.*
>
> 1 Corinthians 3:21-23

"All things are yours"—including the present and future. God's gifts to us include both here and hereafter. The person who attempts to live only for the present will lose the future also. Those who attempt to live only for the future will have no present joy.

12

The Eternal Perspective

The true value of the present and the future will only be perceived by those with a correct perspective. This viewpoint is not the result of solving eschatological riddles. Nor does it come from ignoring either the present or the future. Man is dependent on God for this perspective. The incredible value of this outlook is seen in Hebrews 6. The writer warns of surrendering the priceless joy of tasting "the goodness of the word of God and the powers of the age to come" (Heb. 6:5). Leaving Christ means losing everything, including the ability to evaluate present and future in an integrated way. Thus the writer of Hebrews is saying that for one to maintain allegiance to Christ is also to maintain joyous hope in the "powers of the age to come."

The right perspective integrates our here and now with our future. Another passage in Hebrews develops this idea and demonstrates how the correct viewpoint on eternity helps us continue to make joy-producing decisions in our present life:

These all [Abraham, Sarah, etc.] died in faith, not having received what was promised, but having seen it and greeted it from afar, and having acknowledged that they were strangers and exiles on the earth. For people who speak thus make it clear that they are seeking for a homeland. If they had been thinking of that land from which they had gone out, they would have had opportunity to return. But as it is, they desire a better country, that is, a heavenly one. Therefore God is not ashamed to be called their God, for he has prepared for them a city.

Hebrews 11:13-16

These people made a decision. The promises of the age to come reached down and touched their concrete lives in the present. But leaving their original homeland was not such a loss, either. They left a pagan land to walk with God in a daily life of service. The future as guaranteed by God gave them the ability to evaluate their lives in a new way. They saw themselves from eternity's viewpoint. Without that perspective "they would have had opportunity to return." That is, without this outlook—the combination of present and future from God's view—they would have missed both the joy of earthly pilgrimage with God and future blessings as well. What transformed their present? The affirmation of a future with God!

The Christian's joy is based upon the concreteness of finding God in everyday life as well as in heaven. The restoration of the future, the goal of this book, cannot take place without a restoration of the present. The future can be meaningful only if joy-robbing speculations are abandoned and a present where Christ is dominant is accepted. The future worth having begins here and now with Christ!

---

[1]Hans Kueng, *Signposts of the Future* (Garden City, N.Y.: Doubleday, 1978), p. 14.
[2]Catullus, *Vivamus Mea Lesbia* 5.1–6.

2 Understanding Prophetic Literature

Photography has been my hobby for some time. One of the techniques I learned was the use of filters. For example, a polarization filter can almost eliminate glare. An ultraviolet filter screens out haze. A red filter gives dramatic skies, fleecy clouds, and extra impact to a black-and-white shot. A photographer has to be careful about the kind of filter he uses, because it controls what he gets on the final print.

Biblical interpretation calls for similar caution. An interpreter who rejects miracles on principle uses a filter which makes the supernatural acts of God come out as having a natural explanation. Someone who sees the Bible only as a sourcebook on odd and curious matters, as those who claim God was an early astronaut, will see UFO's on every page. The same principle applies to interpreting Bible prophecy. Thinking of the Bible as a crystal ball is an enormously distorting filter. How can we avoid such faulty presuppositions?

Christ the Center

First must come the key principle of all Bible study—*the centrality of Christ*. We must not impose on the Bible any filter or presupposition which does not glorify Christ and place him at the center of the final picture. Unfortunately, Christ is precisely not the major emphasis of the most popular systems of interpreting prophecy. The major emphasis is upon speculation about world events, time lines, the nation of Israel, and symbolism. This can be seen in the way passages such as Matthew 24 and Mark 13 are handled. We are asked to speculate on a "rapture," various judgments, and intervening events between the return of Christ (*parousia*) and final judgment. But Christ's own emphasis in these key passages is upon faithfulness to him, rather than cleverness. We are to watch for "the son of Man," "the Lord," "the master," "the bridegroom." Who can doubt the center of these eschatological (end-time) statements? It is Christ. Theories of the future which fail to center on Christ are stealing the future.

A second precaution about filters is to be sure that our interpretation on the future is a *realistic extension* of what God has already begun to produce in our present lives. If our vision of the future is a wholly disjointed mishmash of battles, various judgments, second chances, and the like, it should be a warning that we have used the wrong filter. This is why Paul can say "to die is gain" (Phil. 1:21). For Paul, the future must be a consistent extension of a life lived in Christ. The future thus confirms what begins in the present. We cannot have one set of interpretive principles for the here and now, and another for the future.

There is a marvelous consistency in God, and we must interpret his future accordingly. A good example here is the idea about a future state for the faithful on the physical planet earth. If God has already established us as heavenly citizens even here and now (Phil. 3:20), would he *then* consign us to an existence on this here-and-now earth? We must ask, "Do we want the kind of future God has already begun in us, or do we want to make it up as we go along?"

What Did It Mean?

Another important filter is to *determine the passage's meaning for its first readers*. Scripture was not written for a select handful who imagine they live at the end of the world. Imagine the reaction of first century Christians if God had answered their cry for deliverance from persecution with something like, "Don't worry! In about 2,000 years or so I'll begin to get some real interesting things going. There will be a group called the European Common Market, and it will become a new Roman Empire. Then Russia will attack . . . . " Rather, the book of Revelation addressed these early Christians' problems then and there. It told them that God was listening and would begin his judgment of the actions of sinners in the here and now.

Such immediate applications are found in the most seemingly future-oriented books of the Bible. The book of Daniel, for example, is primarily designed to strengthen the faith of those who faced Babylonian opposition. The apocalyptic visions toward the end of the book have primary application to contemporaries of Daniel. The extensive temple prophecies in the latter part of the book of Ezekiel were designed primarily to show the faithful in Ezekiel's time that God is concerned about the integrity of worship. This is quite plain in Ezekiel 44:5-7.

Obviously, scripture may not only have a primary application to those initially addressed, but also an extended or secondary application to those whose situation at any time parallels that of the original hearers. Those on the verge of falling away today need the warnings of the letter to the Hebrews as much as those originally addressed. The powerful example of Daniel and his three friends' faithfulness must have steeled many a Hebrew in the presence of a pagan culture. Even Christians today and in the future can be inspired by the promise, "Those who are wise shall shine like the brightness of the firmament; and those who turn many to righteousness, like the stars for ever and ever" (Dan. 12:3).

Attitudes or Information?

A particularly misleading presupposition in Bible study is the idea that the material exists mainly *to supply information,* especially about the future. The fact is that information about the future is designed to change one's life in the present. In fact, the focus of scripture is not primarily on information, but on the *attitude* expected as a result of the information imparted. The Bible was not written to satisfy human curiosity but to change the human heart. Doctrine is important not for its mere informational value, but to impart to us right ideas about how we can respond to God. The distorting filter of curiosity must be eliminated from our approach to Bible study. No passage more clearly affirms this principle than Deuteronomy 29:29: "The secret things belong to the Lord our God; but the things that are revealed belong to us and to our children for ever, that we may do all the words of this law."

Why Did They Write That Way?

A great deal of Bible prophecy is written in symbolic style. A bit of reflection might help us see why. First, there was in the ancient world an entire class of this type of literature, now often called *apocalyptic*. There was *The Apocalypse of Moses, The Book of Enoch, The Sybilline Oracles* and other such non-canonical books. These books all had certain literary conventions, filled with symbolism, and concerned with victory over oppressors. The New Testament could reach more people if it included a book written in this extremely popular format. God spoke to the people in their own language and respected their own literature. He revealed his truth in such diverse literary styles as poetry, songs, prose, narration, and dialectical conversation. Why should he not reveal truth in a literary form that spoke straight to the heart of the people of that day? What we must do is to investigate the conventions of apocalyptic style to help us understand that form of literature.

Another reason for such literature as the book of Revelation is that symbols are very powerful things. The early Christians lived in a world almost completely dominated by pagan symbolism. That is why Paul's heart was so grieved when he walked through Athens and observed the cultural dominance of paganism on every hand (Acts 17:16). H.

19

B. Swete makes this point in his commentary on the Greet text of Revelation:

> Paganism exercised influence by its complete dominance in literature and art. The Apocalypse is a literary representation of the unseen world—of the future currents of history. Assistance was given to suffering churches by symbolical visions of the majesty of their Divine Lord.[1]

Think of the imagery of Jesus as the Lamb of God slain "from the foundation of the world"; of the great choruses "Worthy is the Lamb . . . " and "Hallelujah"; of the great scenes of victory, saints in white robes washed clean in the blood of the Lamb, the great white throne, the New Jerusalem, the horrors of Babylon the Great, and the lament of the worldly at her fall. The power of these symbols has infused the devotional life of the church. We would be much poorer without their power to suggest and stir up thoughts of the greatness of God and the Lamb.

God Has Your Number

One of the most intriguing areas of symbolism in Bible prophecy deals with numbers. People in the ancient world had a greater respect for numbers than we do. We only connect them with inflation or a raise in pay or something statistical. But from the early geometric efforts of the Nile River farmers through the musings of Pythagoras, numbers fascinated ancient man. The Bible also uses numbers in more than mere statistical ways. When God is said to have the very hairs of our heads numbered, it is something more than a statistic. Jesus says it reflects God's concern about our welfare (Matt. 10:30ff.). When God says to Israel "the cattle on a thousand hills [are mine]" (Ps. 50:10), he is not saying that the livestock on the thousand-and-first hill are somebody else's! It is a poetic way of saying, "All cattle are mine." Notice the next verse of the Psalm: "All that moves in the field is mine." This use of 1,000 to mean a large but indefinite number is somewhat parallel to our saying, "I've told you a thousand times not to exaggerate!" Nobody is counting; it just means a large, indefinite number.

Peter speaks in the same metaphorical way when he says "with the Lord one day is as a thousand years, and a thousand years as one day" (2 Pet. 3:8). He only means that time is not a binding factor on God. When Job says that a person arguing with God could not answer him "once in a thousand times," he does not expect to be successful the thousand-and-first time. Moses' request for a thousand-fold increase of Israel in Deuteronomy 1:11 means only that he desired the nation to grow.

All of this is to prove most helpful as we consider the number 1,000 and its multiples in the book of Revelation. It helps us see that the thousand-year reign spoken of in Revelation 20 cannot be literal—certainly not in this most symbolic of books! Instead it must refer to a long, indefinite period. Thus reflection on the overall biblical use of symbolism in numbers helps specifically with the apocalyptic books. (See chapter 3 for a consideration of other numbers in the Revelation.)

The Joy Robbers

Attention to such principles of interpretation will

help prevent a great deal of confusion in the study of Bible prophecy. The prophetic elements of scripture were not intended to produce confusion, but joy. Jesus promised, "I will see you again, and your hearts will rejoice, and no one will take your joy from you" (John 16:22). But Christ also warned that some would attempt to rob believers of this joy, especially by deceiving them about the future: "For false Christs and false prophets will arise and show great signs and wonders, so as to lead astray, if possible, even the elect" (Matt. 24:24). It is important, therefore, to be aware of systems or theories of prophecy which threaten the confidence, peace, and joy we can rightly have in the here and now.

The interpretive system called "dispensationalism" is one such theory. This is a fairly recent system of biblical interpretation, having originated in the nineteenth century work of John Nelson Darby and the Plymouth Brethren. The major influence in the spread of this system has been the *New Scofield Reference Bible*. The influence of this interpretation has become so widespread that careless onlookers consider it to be *the* conservative approach to prophecy and the future. Yet, the novel complexities of the dispensational approach distort the major emphases of the Bible and choose eschatological fervor rather than testifying to Christ.

The term "dispensationalism" refers to the ages or dispensations in which God's grace is conceived to be at work in special ways. It is assumed that we are now in a dispensation of grace. The dispensation of the kingdom is to begin at the second coming of Christ. We are now living in the dispensation for the Gentiles, and a dispensation for the Jews is yet to come.

What specific joys are we robbed of by dispensational theology? It de-emphasizes Christ's saving work in the present. It emphasizes a God of the future who seems to have little function here and now. The complexity of the system imposes a grid of interpretation upon scripture which negates several important portions of the Bible needed by believers for joyous living. And it leads to disillusionment by setting false dates for the end of time.

The God of the Future

Hal Lindsey says in his book *There's a New World Coming:*

> Even the great church reformers of past centuries, such as Luther, Zwingli, and Calvin, knew little about prophecy. They were primarily interested in unlocking Biblical truths desperately needed for their own generation. They therefore didn't spend much time studying truths about the future.[2]

But were people wrong to concentrate on Bible information needed in their day? Is this not the safest course for the future, to rely on God in the present? By assuming they have the prophetic key, the dispensationalists separate God into two entities, the God of the present and the God of the future. The God of the present is somehow inferior to the God of the future. One merely tries to uncover biblical truth about the present, which is nothing compared to future revelations.

The dispensationalists' view of the book of Revelation is a good indication of this approach. The first three chapters are viewed as a survey of church history up to the present. We are supposedly living now in the Age of Laodicea (indifference) as far as the church is concerned. But then, from chapter four, all is future. All the wonderful scenes of God working in history, the Lamb mediating with his sacrificial blood, the cries of the dead in Christ—all are reserved for some future time. Of course the Bible knows of no such division. If God is not active in the present to hear the cry of the suffering saints, to assure them the struggle must go on for awhile but to keep trusting (Rev. 6:9-11), then all believers are in trouble.

The Golden 'Now'

But, in fact, the stress of scripture is that God is *now*. A golden now runs through the Bible: "Behold, now is the acceptable time; behold, now is the day of salvation" (2 Cor. 6:2). "Today, when you hear his voice, do not harden your hearts . . . " (Heb. 3:7-8). No matter how much ingenuity has gone into creating the system of dispensational interpretation, we are left with the sad feeling that God is strictly the God of the future. That's where all the real action is to take place. Now is only, by their teaching, a parenthesis in prophetic teaching. But if the Bible affirms anything, it affirms a God of the now. Without this, there is no future. Hans Kueng has well said:

> The future cannot be isolated at the expense of the present. The kingdom of God cannot be merely a consoling promise for the future, the satisfaction of pious curiosity about the future, the projection of unfulfilled promises and fears.[3]

Serving the God of the present is the key to the future.

Religious history is littered with the remnants of groups who staked their whole belief systems on someone's wrong-headed prophetic interpretations. Such people either end up totally abandoning faith in God or losing any interest in the Bible. The problem is, of course, that they identified faith in God and biblical teaching with the prophetic wishful thinking of a system. When their system did not deliver, they deluded themselves into believing it was God who did not deliver.

Not When But Who?

The New Testament teaching on the second coming, judgment, and the final resolution of the world is designed to provide joy for the believer, not disappointment. "When?" "Where?" and "How?" are not the right questions to ask. They show our preoccupation with human systems of interpretation. The biblical response to them is to turn the attention toward the one "*who* is to come." The "who" is clearly annunciated. It is this Person upon whom we must center, not the logistics of his arrival. This is the only guarantee of joy—now and future. When we know him, nothing in all the future, not even the last hour, can rob us of joy.

[1]H.B. Swete, *The Apocalypse of St. John,* 3rd ed. (London: Macmillan, 1911), p. cxxxix.

[2]Hal Lindsey, *There's a New World Coming* (Irvine, Calif.: Harvest House Publishers, Inc., 1973), p. 21.

[3]Hans Kueng, op. cit., p. 14.

3 *Interpreting* Revelation

This chapter suggests an interpretive approach to the book of Revelation that is Christ-centered. This book is the most frequently cited source of theories about the future. Sometimes the interpretation is based on what the writer thinks of the "millennium," or thousand-year reign of Christ (Rev. 20:4-5). The *premillennial* view—that Christ's return will be before (pre-) the millennium—requires one approach. The *postmillennial* view—that Christ's return will be after the millennium—results from a second approach. And the *amillennial* view—that there is no real millennium—requires a third approach.

Sometimes the organization of Revelation is along chronological lines. The *preterists* believe that the book deals with a historical situation peculiar to the first century. The *futurist* school, which dominates much Protestant thought today, holds that only Revelation 1-3 are being fulfilled at the present. Chapters 4-22 are generally believed to be composed of events in the future. This is the approach of the dispensationalists. Other ideas are advanced by the *historicists,* who affirm a continuing chronology beginning with the first century. For them, Revelation predicted such events as the Islamic invasions of the seventh century A.D., the French Revolution, and World War II.

Still other ways to approach the book are suggested by those not interested in chronology. The spiritualizers, philosophy of history symbolists, or cycle of history interpreters emphasize mastering the symbolic content of Revelation. Sections of the book are often understood to depict cycles of persecution and judgment throughout history. For example, the seven trumpets are a cycle which is paralleled in the seven bowls of wrath, but with more intensity.

Perhaps something good can be said for certain aspects of each of these interpretations. Certainly some events in Revelation are in the future, some have already occurred, and others happen in cycles. There is much symbolism to be comprehended, and an overall viewpoint can be most helpful. Still, if only one system is applied exclusively the book can become seriously distorted. The danger is that the system may become greater than the book, forcing the material to fit the presuppositions of the interpreter.

Are there other possibilities? Does Revelation itself suggest a better approach? I believe that it does give a significant clue to a viewpoint that proves to be more adequate than a millennial or a chronological interpretation. This viewpoint will also give more coherence to the symbols and cycles employed. I believe that Revelation suggests that *the person and work of Christ* is the organizing principle of greatest importance in understanding its message.

Jesus, the Spirit of Prophecy

In Revelation 19 a significant episode displays the heart of the book's prophetic interest. John listens to the sublime choruses of praise and realizes that God's saints will triumph. Jesus' church will share with him at the marriage supper of the Lamb. When the angelic guide tells John of the triumphant future, he is overwhelmed and falls at the feet of the angel. The angel rejects John's worshipful posture and says sharply:

> Watch out, don't do this! I am a fellow servant with you and your brethren who have the testimony of Jesus. Worship God! For the testimony of Jesus is the spirit of prophecy. *
>
> Revelation 19:10

Worship is to be directed toward God, not angels, because of "the testimony of Jesus." It is this testimony that is the heart and soul of Revelation. It is the very "spirit of prophecy."

The testimony of Jesus. Does the "testimony of Jesus" mean Jesus' own testimony, or the testimony *about* Jesus? Most commentators believe the former. But this is not a crucial question. Jesus certainly testified of God to man, but he also is the object of that testimony, for the saving acts of Jesus are the center of both Gospel and Revelation (cf. Rev. 1:5; 5:9; 7:14). H.B. Swete says, "all true prophets are witnesses of Jesus."[1] G.B. Caird connects this testimony with the "faithful witness" theme about Jesus in 1:5 and 3:14 and comments that "the Spirit speaks to the churches in the accents of the crucified and risen Lord."[2] Prophecy, as used in the book of Revelation, centers on Jesus Christ. Jacques Ellul, the French scholar, strongly

28

reinforces this viewpoint as he speaks of the theme of the book:

> Its theological theme could be summed up in the revelation that Jesus Christ is master of history: it does not at all contrast a bad present with a good future; it reveals the *present* work of God, it shows the *present* victory of Jesus Christ.[3]

The nature of prophecy. Predictive elements do not have lives of their own in the Revelation. Its prophecies exist only to show the comprehensive activities of the Son of God. Actually, prophecy is not primarily prediction; it is proclamation. The word is from the verb *prophēmi,* "I speak forth." The Arndt-Gingrich lexicon defines the related verb *prophēteuo* as meaning to: (1) proclaim a divine revelation; (2) reveal what is hidden; and only then, (3) foretell the future.[4] The major thrust of true prophecy is to proclaim the Lord's saving acts, not to predict the future. Even the predictive elements in such a proclamation are subordinate to the major emphasis. Thus the prophetic impact of Revelation is to reveal Jesus Christ.

When the message from Jesus and about Jesus dominates our proclamation we have what prophecy in Revelation is all about. On this basis, the scenes in which Christ appears, or in which his appearance leads to some action, should form an internal outline of the book. In fact, five significant appearances by Christ do form the heart of the work. As described by John, Jesus appears as (1) the faithful witness (ch. 1); (2) the Lord of the churches (chs. 2–3); (3) the Lamb of God (chs. 4–11); (4) the victorious Word of God (chs. 12–20); and (5) the coming Christ (chs. 21–22).

29

The Faithful Witness

The word "witness" is from the Greek word *martus* (cf. martyr) and means "one who testifies." Jesus is the prime witness, the one whose testimony about God resulted in his death. The book opens with a declaration that it is "the revelation of Jesus Christ" (1:1). No doubt Jesus possesses the revelation from God, but he is also that revelation itself, since the book's contents center on him. The book is called a book of prophecy (1:3), but it is prophecy that reveals the faithfulness of Jesus Christ. This is why the first description of Jesus is that of the "faithful witness" (1:5). Jesus is the prototype for all those who must continue their faithfulness to the testimony of God. Readers are to begin the book impressed with how the faithfulness of Jesus has blessed them. In him they have love, release from sins, and new status as a kingdom of priests (1:5-6).

Because of his loyalty, Jesus is called the "first-born of the dead and the ruler of the kings of the earth" (1:5). This sets up the triple theme that runs throughout the book: God's people share in Jesus' *faithfulness, life,* and *sovereignty.* If his people read this book looking for that which promotes these three objectives, they will be delivered from expecting to find only esoteric, future surprises.

The next vision that John shares describes this three-fold work of Christ in the context of Jesus walking in the midst of his churches (congregations).

The Lord of the Churches

The churches of John's day were threatened by persecutors from without and dangers from within.

They needed to know that Christ was aware of their struggles and cared about them. Some who were yielding to the pressures of the surrounding paganism needed stern warnings from the Head of the church to stiffen their resolve. The vision of Christ in chapter 1 sets the tone for Christ's involvement with his church (chs. 1–3). In this vision Christ is seen as the great High Priest. John is impressed with his majesty and authority. Yet, when he speaks, it is the Jesus John knew upon the earth. He has conquered death and lives to help his disciples deal with their fears.

But another important emphasis comes to the fore. Jesus is the Christ of the churches. John sees him walking in the midst of "seven golden lampstands" (1:13) which symbolize the churches (1:20). As G. B. Caird perceptively notes: "The first characteristic of Christ revealed to John in his vision is that he is present among the earthly congregations of his people."[5] Christ is not remotely directing activities from heaven. He continues to be intimately associated with his church.

Letters to the Seven Churches

The letters to the seven churches grow out of this vision of Christ in the middle of the seven lampstands. The vision supplies the attributes of Christ that are mentioned in the opening lines of each individual letter. The divine virtues of Jesus qualify him to speak to his churches. Each virtue is mentioned to help the different congregations deal with their specific needs. Christ is suggesting that *to know him better* is to begin to solve their problems. Churches of our day could learn this lesson to great profit. We need to know Christ better if we are to deal with our needs!

The church at Ephesus, for example, needed to know that the church is Christ's, not theirs. Therefore they are told that Christ is the one holding the seven stars and walking among the seven golden lampstands (2:1). The Ephesians were most sound, but they did not love as they had at one time. Christ controls his church by love, and the Ephesians must learn that quickly or else they will lose their standing as a church of Christ (2:5). In the same way Christ shares his attributes with the other congregations that they might find the resources that would deliver them.

The second feature of the letters to the churches stresses Jesus' intimate knowledge of their circumstances. He knows of their works and labor: that Ephesus is diligent but unloving; that Sardis has completed none of its projects of faith. He knows of the affliction of Smyrna, the love of Thyatira, the lukewarmness of Laodicea. Jesus' continued nearness is seen in his awareness. Today, Revelation speaks to us in the same accents. Jesus *knows!*

The third stage in each letter is a promise to the conqueror. Jesus is revealing that he stands behind his promises. The struggle will be most worthwhile. Since the promises come from the Faithful Witness, they may be depended upon. Thus in three ways the Christ of the churches continues reaching out to his people. Revelation is telling us that Jesus—the qualified, knowing, and sharing Jesus—is still close to his church.

The Lamb of God

A sudden shift in perspective begins in chapter 4

of Revelation. But even here Christ continues to occupy central place. The scene is now heaven, far above the struggle and strife of the churches on earth. The scene is now being set for the revelation of the Lamb of God. Christ has been shown to be walking amid the churches on earth. Now he is shown to be in the very center of the throneroom of the Father himself: "And between the throne and the four living creatures and among the elders, I saw a Lamb standing, as though it had been slain" (5:6). Though the scene on earth is confused, heaven is tranquil. God is in complete control. But how shall the prophetic word of God's plan be opened for those strugglers on earth? How may they also share in the peace of heaven? Only through the worthiness of the Lamb. Only the Lamb can open God's plan and show his redemption and judgment to those upon the earth. He alone is worthy because he has accepted death to benefit those in need of God's grace:

> Worthy art thou to take the scroll
>   and to open its seals,
> for thou wast slain and by thy
>   blood didst ransom men for
>   God
> from every tribe and tongue and
>   people and nation,
> and hast made them a kingdom
>   and priests to our God,
> and they shall reign on earth.
>
> Revelation 5:9-10

God's plan for mankind is realized only through the death of Christ. It would all be a closed book without Jesus.

Whatever will be known about the currents of redemption in our history will be known through the worthiness of the slain Lamb of God. Certainly this affirms Christ crucified to be the heart of the prophetic revelation. When the lamb begins to open the seven seals, he reveals that the church will carry on its ministry in a world where history is often threatening. A remarkable correspondence is found in Jesus' discourse in Matthew 24:3ff: There will be "wars and rumors of wars," "famines," and "earthquakes." "But the end is not yet" (24:6) for the church must bear testimony in the midst of ongoing history. The Lamb reveals this, for his sacrifice was made in history, not at the end of history.

It will be observed that much of the subsequent development of the book grows out of the Lamb's ability to open the seven seals. The seals lead to the warning trumpet judgments and subsequently to the bowls of wrath.

We see here also Christ as the Preserver of the Church. Throughout eras of history when periods of persecution are followed by consequent acts of judgment by God, the church is shielded by the Lamb. This is a subsequent theme developing out of the key scene in chapter 5. Both the vision of those sealed on earth in chapter 7 (the church at any given moment in history) and the great innumerable multitude in heaven (7:9ff.) owe their salvation to God and the Lamb (7:10). The hymn of thanksgiving in 7:14-15 shows that continued reliance on the blood of Jesus is the key to surviving the pressures on the church. The Lamb preserves his people through the cycles of persecution.

The Victorious Word of God

This complex theme begins in chapter 12. God institutes a decisive act which leads to the complete defeat of all evil. The devil and his allies suffer a crushing blow which works out in chapters 12–20. The victory begins with an event which might be considered insignificant if we read the book with something in mind other than "the testimony of Jesus is the spirit of prophecy." But it is the key to the inevitable defeat of all hostile powers. The great event is the incarnation of Jesus!

> And a great portent appeared in heaven, a woman clothed with the sun, with the moon under her feet, and on her head a crown of twelve stars; she was with child and she cried out in her pangs of birth, in anguish for delivery . . . She brought forth a male child, one who is to rule all the nations with a rod of iron, but her child was caught up to God and to his throne.
>
> Revelation 12:1-2

John's subsequent treatment shows that the "woman" is not strictly Mary, but rather the covenant community which brings the Messiah into the world. This covenant community, which *after* the ascension flees "into the wilderness," is the church.

Chapter 12:7 and what follows shows the pivotal importance of the incarnation of the Christ. The accusing work of the devil is ended. He and his forces are routed. Thus, the acceptance of humanity by Christ is seen as the prime cause of the devil's defeat: "Now the salvation and the power and the kingdom of our God and the authority of his Christ have come, for the accuser of our brethren has been thrown down" (12:10).

As Jesus himself confirmed, this defeat of Satan began in history, not at the end of history: "The seventy returned with joy, saying 'Lord, even the demons are subject to us in your name!' And he said to them, 'I saw Satan fall like lightning from heaven' " (Luke 10:17-18). The defeat of Satan is inaugurated by the first coming of Christ; it is consummated by the second. This theme forms the substance of Revelation 12–20. The defeat of Satan, the world empire in alliance with him (13:1ff.), the false ideologies that support Satan's ally (13:11), and whatever other powers oppose God's purposes, all follow the incarnation, the coming of Christ into the world.

Jesus, whom Satan could not destroy, now carries out the successful warfare against the archenemy. John describes Jesus in Revelation 19:13 as the "Word of God." Referring back to 19:10, our key text, "the testimony of Jesus is the spirit of prophecy," we realize he is the Word of God that conquers. The defeat of evil is actualized by holding onto the word of Jesus. Thus prophecy points to God's victory as accomplished only by the Word of God. Crystal ball gazers do not defeat Satan; only those "faithful and true" to the gospel can share in this victory (19:11). This leads us to realize also that 20:1-10 is not about the millennium at all, but about the defeat of Satan. Satan, first restricted, then destroyed, is brought to defeat by the Word of God.

Christ, the Coming One

The fifth appearance of Christ in Revelation is as the coming one. The Lamb of God is our guarantee of the eternal presence of God (21:22-23). The readers of Revelation are thus confronted with a choice. The choice is not whether to accept this or that theory of the end time, but whether to accept Christ, the coming one! This is the impact that should come from studying Revelation! (See 22:14-21.) "He who testifies to these things says, 'Surely I am coming soon.' Amen. Come, Lord Jesus!" (22:20).

"He who *testifies*" is Jesus. In other words, the entire book has been a testimony of Jesus. No wonder he occupies the central position in the five scenes we have described! Understanding Jesus' testimony as the very spirit of prophecy delivers us from strange theories and helps us embrace the saving work of Christ. Christ is revealed as the Faithful Witness who can thus inspire our faithfulness; as The Lord constantly present with his church; as the Lamb of God who preserves his people through struggle; as the victorious Word of God whose incarnation spelled defeat for evil; and as the Coming One whose arrival consummates every blessing and ends all evil.

Come, Lord Jesus!

---

[1] H.B. Swete, op. cit., p. 249.

[2] G.B. Caird, *The Revelation of St. John the Divine* (New York: Harper-Row Publications, 1966), p. 238.

[3] Jacques Ellul, *Apocalypse: The Book of Revelation,* Crossroad Books, (New York: Seabury Press, 1977), p. 31.

[4] W. F. Arndt and F. W. Gingrich, *A Greek-English Lexicon of the New Testament,* (Chicago: University of Chicago Press, 1957), p. 730.

[5] G. B. Caird, op. cit., p. 25.

4 Finding the Kingdom

As an undergraduate, I was a member of our debate team. One tournament I remember was held at Harvard University. At the banquet, which was part of the activities, the Harvard Debate Club had invited a prominent attorney to speak on the issues of the day. I don't remember much he said except that the government reminded him of a log floating down the river with a million ants crawling all over it. "And," he concluded, "every ant thinks he's running the log."

Things do appear to be out of control at times. Chaos would look organized compared to some of the incredible confusion in our world. The real shame is that people's lives are about as confused as the world. We need an organizing center. Something is needed to pull us together, not to further confuse us. In other words, somebody needs to be in charge.

Now this is what I believe is the basic idea in the concept the Bible calls "the kingdom of God." The kingdom of God means God is in charge and those who have their lives organized around him have moved from confusion to certainty. The kingdom of God is composed of his subjects—those who have made his Son Jesus Lord of their lives. There are no territorial limits to this kingdom, for it is not so much a place as a style of life—the style of a servant doing the will of the King, with joy.

Confusion About the Kingdom

Running into the phrase "kingdom of God" in a good bit of contemporary religious literature is like running into a revolving door. For now there are those threatening to make chaos out of the one, solid organizing idea needed in our era of confusion! The whole issue has degenerated into debating about the identity of the kingdom, whether it is past, present, or future, whether it is heavenly or on the earth, whether it is the church or the millennium.

Is this ongoing semantic battle the reason God introduced the idea of the kingdom? Of course not. God is much more positive about the kingdom than most men have been. He has something specific in mind with this idea, a heartening experience for his people. John's opening thoughts in Revelation center on this encouraging affirmation about the kingdom:

> To him who loves us and has freed us from our sins by his blood and made us a kingdom, priests to his God and Father, to him be glory and dominion for ever and ever. Amen.
>
> Revelation 1:5b-6

Whatever else "kingdom" may mean, it is certainly something to be thankful about. It is obviously closely connected with the love, forgiveness, and service of God in Jesus Christ.

Cutting Through the Confusion

There are many complex speculations about the kingdom. In reading about them one cannot help wonder if some of the simplicity Jesus demonstrated in talking about the kingdom has been lost. "The kingdom of heaven is like this . . . ," Jesus would say, and then tell of fields sown with good and bad seed, of nets dragging in all sorts of fish, of bad men killing the son of the vineyard owner, and of other such homely illustrations. Something profound yet simple has been lost.

Then consider how Paul cut through the confusion in exactly the same way in Romans 14. Christians were sure the kingdom of God meant arguing over whether to eat meat or vegatables, and whether to respect one day as holier than another. Paul cut through this complex gordian knot by saying:

> The kingdom of God is not food and drink but righteousness and peace and joy in the Holy Spirit; he who thus serves Christ is acceptable to God and approved by men. Let us then pursue what makes for peace and mutual upbuilding.
>
> Romans 14:17-19

Like John in Revelation 1:5-6, the kingdom is shown to deal with realities and attitudes possible only when God is in charge of lives. Pilate, the political appointee from Rome, had a more adequate idea of what the concept was all about than many latter day interpreters. Pilate asked Jesus point blank: "Are you the King of the Jews?" (John 18:33). Isn't this the central question? Pilate wanted to know if Jesus considered himself *to be in charge*. Jesus' answer is equally focused:

> "My kingship is not of this world; if my kingship were of this world, my servants would fight . . . but my kingship is not from the world." Pilate said to him, "So you are a king?" Jesus answered, "You say that I am a king. For this I was born, and for this I have come into the world, to bear witness to the truth. Every one who is of the truth hears my voice."
>
> John 18:36-37

Now we see that the concept of the kingdom also includes a primary commitment to square one's life with the truth. This is obviously no power play, no military sovereignty, but a centering on the truth of God.

Defining the Kingdom

When Jesus refers to his "kingship" in John 18:36 he uses the word *basileia,* usually translated "kingdom" in most other passages in the Bible. The word means *reign* rather than *realm*. Arndt and Gingrich, in their scholarly lexicon of New Testament Greek, define the term to mean 1. kingship; 2. royal power; 3. royal rule; 4. kingdom. The major stress in the word is living under the reign of the king. Those in the kingdom are those in whose lives God is reigning. George E. Ladd describes the kingdom this way:

> The kingdom of God is the sovereign rule of God, manifested in the person and work of Christ, creating a people over whom he reigns, and issuing in a realm or realms in which the power of his reign is realized.[1]

41

The clearing of the confusion then is evident. The question "Who's in charge?" is answered. The kingdom of God is not a concept to debate; it is God ruling in our lives. It is an assurance of God's reign, now and forever. This gives the direction we need. Now, where shall we find the kingdom of God?

The works of John Nelson Darby, Lewis S. Chafer, and Charles Ryrie generally affirm that Jesus offered the "Davidic kingdom" to the Jews. When they refused, according to this dispensational theory, God postponed the kingdom until the millennial reign and instituted the idea of the church. The church is supposed to be a "mystery parenthesis" not described in prophetic works nor in any way identified with the kingdom of God. Thus one could not say the kingdom was present today, according to these concepts. It could only be a future hope.

Of course, according to the preceding definition of the kingdom, this system of interpretation really says that God is not ruling in the lives of people in the present age. This is simply not true. The church is the present manifestation of the kingdom of God. This is amply illustrated in both prophetic as well as non-prophetic biblical literature.

The Evidence from Daniel

A king's dream in the book of Daniel forecasts that Christ's kingdom was *not* to be postponed until his second coming, as we often hear. Instead, it was to be established in the days of the late Roman empire. The king had dreamed of an enormous image made of four strata of metals. The head was gold, the breast and arms were silver, the belly and thighs bronze, the legs iron, and the feet "partly of iron and partly of clay" (Dan. 2:33). The prophet Daniel interpreted the dream. Each of the metal sections represented a kingdom, he said. The first, the head of gold, represented Nebuchadnezzar's own kingdom, Babylon (Dan. 2:37-38). The other kingdoms follow each other *in historical connection*. We can conclude from world history that the other kingdoms are as follows: silver—Medo-Persian; bronze—Grecian; iron—Roman; and iron and clay—late Roman (a "divided kingdom," Dan. 2:41).

In the king's dream a stone was cut out "by no human hand" and used to strike down the monster image, scattering it far and wide. "But the stone that struck the image became a great mountain and filled the whole earth " (Dan. 2:35). Daniel says of this stone:

> And in the days of those kings [the ones represented by mingled iron and clay] the God of heaven will set up a kingdom which shall never be destroyed, nor shall its sovereignty be left to another people. It shall break in pieces all these kingdoms and bring them to an end, and it shall stand forever; just as you saw that a stone was cut from a mountain by no human hand . . . .
>
> Daniel 2:44-45a

Now, it would be impossible, as dispensationalists affirm, that this kingdom is to be set up at the last advent of Christ. The reason is evident when we read the whole prophecy, for the stone strikes the image while it is still *in one piece*. The only way the image can be in one piece is if the four empires are considered as still in historical connection. Tracing world history through the above kingdoms proves that the church described in the New Testament, in the late Roman empire, is the "kingdom which shall never be destroyed." This is so because there is no other historical succession possible if we begin with the Babylonian empire.

Thus, to make the image's feet refer to a "revived Roman empire," at the end of the world as we know it, is to miss the point of the prophecy totally. Daniel said God's reign would be established while the continuity of these four empires was a historical reality. Therefore, Christ's kingdom was prophesied to begin in the days of Rome. Those familiar with Acts 2 realize this is exactly what happened. As the Bible scholar F. F. Bruce states:

> In Jesus' ministry the Kingdom of God was in process of inauguration. With His death and resurrection, followed by the descent of the Spirit, this process was completed. The Kingdom has now been inaugurated: in Jesus' words, it has "come with power" (Mark 9:1).[2]

Believers Are in the Kingdom Now

This is why Paul is able to say in his letter to the Colossians that our deliverance from sin means that we are now under God's reign, that we are in the kingdom now: "He has delivered us from the dominion of darkness and transferred us to the *kingdom* of his beloved Son, in whom we have redemption, the forgiveness of sin" (Col. 1:13-14). To have God in charge is to be forgiven and loved. This is precisely what Christ offered, and still offers. It is this *present* kingdom emphasis that can bring order out of chaos in our lives. The church is the present phase of God's reign. The kingdom of God was not postponed to the millennium, as dispensationalists say. We can have God in charge of our lives here and now—and what a joy that is!

But what of the kingdom's future? Is the kingdom to have a thousand-year earthly phase? Will it mean living in the earthly city of Jerusalem and having Christ literally reigning in person for that period of time? What is the future of the kingdom?

Our Citizenship Is in Heaven

God has given believers citizenship in heaven, even in this life. We know this is not the earth, for it is where Christ is presently (Phil. 3:21). When Christ comes we will undergo a change to be able to live that heavenly life. The Bible does not teach us that God plans to consign believers to this earth when Christ comes. Actually, land promises are for this life, not the life to come. When Peter tells Jesus he has left everything to follow him, Jesus replies:

> Truly, I say to you, there is no one who has left house or brothers or sisters or mother or father or children or lands, for my sake and for the gospel, who will not receive a hundredfold now in this time, houses and brothers and sisters and mothers and children and lands, with persecution, and in the age to come eternal life.
>
> Mark 10:29-30

God blesses us in this time with such wonderful relationships as a whole new family when we become Christians. He also provides for our material needs. Many believers could testify to the generous gift of houses, lands, and other blessings to meet their needs. But, according to Jesus, the age to come is to see the fruition of eternal life, not the continuance of more lands and houses!

What About the Millennium?

But what about the doctrine of the millennium in Revelation 20? Does it not teach a thousand-year reign with Christ on the earth? A brief look at this passage (Rev. 20:1-6) is enough to make one wonder about the origin of all the ideas supposedly in it. What is *not* said is quite astounding:

• The location of the reign with Christ
• The word "earth"
• The land of Palestine
• Jews
• The antichrist

The only way to be fair with this passage is to discuss what *is* mentioned.

An exegesis of Revelation 20:1-6 must begin with the realization that the primary theme is the defeat of the last of God's enemies, the devil. The monster and the false prophet's doom have already been mentioned (Rev. 19:20). Now it is Satan's turn, first to be curtailed, then to be completely vanquished.

The second consideration is to deal with the literalness of the passage. Those who question an earthly millennium are often chided for not taking the passage literally. But is there anyone who takes *everything* here literally? All commentators are quite selective in what they take to be literal.

Those who take the one thousand years to be quite literal do not feel any obligation to take Satan to be a literal dragon. Nor do they insist he will be bound with a physical chain or cast into a real hole in the ground. It would be hard for anyone to conceive of this sort of binding being effective on a spiritual being. Also, it is difficult to see how the "souls" of beheaded believers could literally be seen by the apostle (vs. 4).

One thousand is used symbolically a number of times in the Bible, e.g. Deut. 1:11; Job 9:3; Psalm 50:10; and, of course, the "thousand years as one day" passage in 2 Peter 3:8. If one thousand years could be used symbolically in a book like 2 Peter, why could not the most symbolical book in the Bible use it the same way? Thus, it would seem that the thousand years refers to a long indefinite time when deceased saints will not be defeated by Satan and death but will actually be reigning with Christ as they await the final defeat of Satan.

A third point to be dealt with is whether the passage says that this thousand-year reign is to be upon the earth. H. B. Swete notes in his commentary on the Greek text of Revelation that "upon the earth" (*epi tēs gēs*) has no place either in verse 4 or verse 6 "and must not be read between the lines."[3]

A fourth point is that the mention of "thrones" here is a strong indication that heaven, not earth, is intended. Leon Morris observes:

Those who see a literal millennium usually place them [thrones] on earth. But John does not say this. He uses "throne" forty-seven times in all, and except for Satan's throne

(2:13) and that of the beast (13:2; 16:10) all appear to be in heaven.[4]

The only possible explanation that does not add a whole new set of ideas to the text is to assume that John is not talking about an earthly kingdom at all. He is saying that Satan will not defeat those who die for Christ. The dead in Christ will reign with him for a long period of time while Satan's activities are curtailed with respect to "deceiving the nations." We hold that period to be now, for the very means to curtail Satan's activities among the nations is to carry the gospel to "all the nations" as Jesus instructs in Matthew 28:19ff. Satan did not defeat those who suffered for Christ. He only succeeded in placing them in a situation which is "far better" (Phil. 1:23).

God's kingdom has a future, but it is not on this earth. The reign of God will continue through all eternity (1 Cor. 15:24; 2 Tim. 4:18; 2 Pet. 1:11). Heaven will see the realization of its potential.

What a Difference the Kingdom Makes!

Joy comes to us in realizing that our chaotic lives can find direction under God's reign. We do not have to wait for some millennial reign to experience the leadership of our God. God wants us to be in his kingdom now. But what practical effect should this have on our lives?

Although being in the kingdom assures us that our lives will not disintegrate into chaos, it is not a realm in which there are no challenges. If the King blesses us with order, he also has the authority to order our lives. Hence, life in the kingdom is of the highest ethical order. Jesus is clear about this in the Sermon on the Mount. (This context is significant—it is in Matthew's gospel, which has been called "the gospel of the kingdom.") "Unless your righteousness exceeds that of the scribes and Pharisees," Jesus warns, "you will never enter the kingdom of heaven" (Matt. 5:20).

It is in the kingdom, therefore, that we learn about "second mile religion," turning the other cheek, loving our enemies, and refraining not only from murder and adultery but from hatred and lust. In a sense, the entire Sermon on the Mount, which enjoins such standards on the King's subjects, can be thought of as the kingdom's constitution and by-laws. When those in the kingdom rise to these challenges, they raise a standard or sign which proclaims that the kingdom is present in the here and now. If consistently practiced by citizens of the kingdom, these ethics of the kingdom would revolutionize human relationships.

But, as we would expect of a loving king, the *blessings* of living under his rule far outweigh the responsibilities. Again in Matthew's kingdom-gospel, the beatitudes (Matt. 5:1-12) indicate the blessedness—perhaps we might say the *peculiar* blessedness—which describes those who are in the kingdom. For this famous passage turns upside down the value systems of other realms. Not the proud but the poor in spirit possess the kingdom of heaven. The mournful, the meek, those who hunger and thirst after righteousness, the merciful, the pure in heart, the peacemakers, the persecuted—these kinds of people receive the practical, day-to-day assurance that they possess the kingdom of God.

Further, those who truly put the kingdom first in their lives are even to be provided their physical needs: "Seek first his kingdom and his righteousness, and all these things [food and clothing] shall be yours as well" (Matt. 6:33). Thus, a new Christian, struggling to make his way through college, decides to make his regular church contribution even though he does not know where next week's groceries are coming from. And in the next day's mail is a check—his uncle had sold the young man's saddle, which he had forgotten about. The money for groceries was there. Life in the kingdom, though involving risk and daring, is always rewarding in some way.

Finally, we can notice that the everyday life of citizens of the kingdom is undergirded with an optimistic view of life unmatched by the kingdoms of the world. As chapter 6 will show more fully, the outcome of the Christian's struggle with evil has already been assured by Christ's victory over death. Therefore, even in the midst of sorrow or pain, we can borrow from the deposit of hope and optimism already credited to our account by the victory won by Jesus. Once more we see that being in the kingdom does not mean postponing joy until the future. We live triumphantly through everyday difficulties because we know that the kingdom's major battle has already been fought and won by none other than the King himself!

---

[1]George E. Ladd, *Crucial Questions About the Kingdom of God* (Grand Rapids, Mich.: Eerdmans Publishing Company, 1952), p. 113.
[2]F. F. Bruce, *God's Kingdom and Church* (Grand Rapids, Mich.: Eerdmans Publishing Company, 1978), p. 134.
[3]H. B. Swete, op. cit., p. 264.
[4]Leon Morris, *The Revelation of St. John* (Grand Rapids, Mich.: Eerdmans Publishing Company, 1969), p. 236.

5 *Living in the* Last Days

Bible writers attach great practical importance to Christ's return—the *parousia* (pah-roo-SEE-ah). The particular emphases in Scripture are on the attitudes and actions which are appropriate to Christ's return. These attitudes and actions, which are to be practiced in our here-and-now existence, are (1) responsibility, (2) alertness, and (3) confident hope.

The Persons We Ought To Be

Even casual consideration of the New Testament doctrine of Christ's return will impress the reader with its practicality. There is no hint of speculative fancies; all is exceedingly attitude-oriented. Peter, for example, develops the enormously powerful doctrine of the destruction of the present world order in chapter 3 of his second letter. He mixes no speculation into the thought, but instantly shares this practical insight with his readers:

> Since all these things are thus to be dissolved, what sort of persons ought you to be in lives of holiness and godliness, waiting for

51

and hastening the coming of the day of God.

2 Peter 3:11-12

A similar development is found in Paul's lengthy passage on the parousia in 1 Thessalonians. Many scholars feel that this letter may be Paul's earliest extant letter. It was written to a young congregation of new converts. They had become confused on the doctrine of the return of Christ, and Paul writes to clarify the issue. If ever there was a time when an apostle would stress what was of central importance to the Christian in the second appearance of Christ, it would be now. Paul opens his clarification by stating that his purpose is "that you may not grieve as others who have no hope" (4:13). The reason they may have hope is that whether they are alive or not when the Lord returns, they will suffer no loss, or as Paul says, "so we shall always be with the Lord" (4:17). The conclusion of the first point ends, "Therefore comfort one another with these words" (4:18).

Paul then takes up the theme of how the second appearance is to serve as an incentive to moral excellence. But first he has a severe warning about trying to figure out the "times and seasons" of Christ's return. "For you yourselves know well that the day of the Lord will come like a thief in the night" (5:2). On the basis of that warning, Paul proceeds with exhortations to alertness and seriousness of purpose. Not one statement in this entire section hints of the kind of speculative treatment accorded the second coming of Christ in so much religious literature today. The apostolic use of this doctrine is obviously encouraging and ethical in nature.

Responsible at His Coming

Christ's coming teaches his people to be aware of their responsibilities. The responsible enter into the "joy of the Lord" (Matt. 24:45 ff; 25:21; 25:23; 25:26f.; 25:31ff.). Lazy, irresponsible discipleship cheats us of the present joy of active service. It also clouds our future with the Lord, for he cannot bless the person who has not enough interest to invest his entire being in serving Chirst. As Jesus phrases it:

> Who then is the faithful and wise servant, whom his master has set over his household, to give them their food at the proper time? Blessed is that servant whom his master when he comes will find so doing. Truly, I say to you, he will set him over all his possessions.
>
> Matthew 24:45-47

Serious Discipleship

The idea of the end of all things earthly has often spurred retreat from the world. Mention has been made of those who thought they had the end of the world figured out and who subsequently left society and waited for the Lord to come. The New Testament actually takes the opposite approach. Instead of recommending "getting away from it all" because of the possibility of Christ's return, New Testament writers counsel even more intense commitment to each other. The idea of the end encourages serious discipleship, not retreat. Peter, for example, says:

> The end of all things is at hand; therefore keep sane and sober for your prayers. Above

all hold unfailing your love for one another,
since love covers a multitude of sins. Practice
hospitality ungrudgingly to one another. As
each has received a gift, employ it for one
another.

1 Peter 4:7-10

Peter, like Jesus, enforces the idea that at Christ's
return we are to be found doing our duty. The finite
end to the age cannot be urged as a call to abandon
ministry. Keeping "sane and sober" in a devotional
relationship with the Lord is the best attitude from
which to minister. As Peter points out, the thought
of the Lord's return is to be motivation for a love
that does not dissipate.

Love is what motivated Christ to be responsible
in his own ministry. Paul points to this in his great
discussion of ministry in 2 Corinthians 5. He begins by discussing the appearance he will make
before the Lord when he is "at home" with him
(5:9). This reminds Paul of his accountability to the
Lord (vs. 10). The "fear" or respect that he feels
toward the Lord motivates him to act responsibly
with his ministry, to "persuade men" in the action
of sharing the gospel (vs. 11).

Then Paul reveals his most basic motive for responsible service. It is the "love of Christ" which
now controls his actions and ministry. He realizes
that Christ has demonstrated the ultimate responsibility by dying for all (vss. 14-15). This great action
of Christ now controls Paul's life. He began by not
wanting to disappoint the Lord and ends by being
utterly controlled by the Lord's sacrificial love.
This is the way the responsible disciple will always
progress. He may begin by "doing his duty"; but if
he truly appreciates the Lord, it is not long until

the Lord's love moves into utter control of his life. Responsibility is love in motion.

Alert at His Coming

There exists an inordinate need for alertness in our society. Inter-continental ballistic missiles are only twenty minutes from our cities. An elaborate defense network stands ready to alert the citizens of the United States. Similarly, we have home fire warning systems, tornado alerts, and winter weather warnings. We can discern the signs of politics, warfare, and weather, but can we discern the signs of the times? Are we alert to what really matters? The second coming of the Lord stresses the need for alertness on the part of his followers. Many passages on the coming of Christ stress this thought (see Matt. 24:42f.; 25:13; 1 Thess. 5:1-11).

The kind of alertness encouraged by the New Testament is not anxious and frantic. It is urgency under control. Competent Christians are those who sense the real urgency of being alert for Christ in this present age. Yet, they are not out of control, frantic, or frenetic.

This sense of controlled urgency was impressed upon me recently when a bright vacation day nearly became a personal tragedy. I was in Florida with my family when my boy and I decided to fish off the rocks. As I was moving along the rocks near the water's edge, I suddenly slipped and tumbled backwards into the ocean.

The waves kept dragging me out toward the sea, so I reached out for the rocks. I failed to notice that implanted in them were rows of razor-sharp barnacle shells. As I clutched at the rocks frantically for a handhold, the barnacles sliced deeply into my right hand. A bright stream of blood began to flow rapidly from my hand. Ignoring that unnerving sight I finally scrambled up the rocks and pulled myself ashore. Taking out my wet handkerchief I fashioned a makeshift compress and headed toward our apartment half a mile up the shore, with my son helping me along.

Soon my wife Joyce had me in the car and headed for the local hospital. The receiving nurse was calm, but alert. "Been into the barnacles I see," she noted as she quickly washed and sterilized the wound. The whole atmosphere was efficiently urgent. The doctor proceeded to stitch up the wound with skill and patience. There was no anxiety, yet everyone did their job promptly and professionally. Their behavior built up my confidence. I would not have wanted them to have become so unglued that their attitude would have suggested concerned incompetence.

Likewise, no frantic whirligigs are going to get on with the urgent task of winning a world to Jesus. They'll be too busy running around the circular track of their own confusion to help anyone. Perhaps that is why the biblical teaching on alertness at the coming of Christ also often stresses seriousness of purpose. (See 1 Thess. 5:6.)

Being 'On Alert'

I spent ten years in the U. S. Marine Corps. It all started when some friends suggested one peaceful day in 1949 that we all join the Marine Corps Reserve. "They give you free uniforms and pay you to attend drills right in your hometown," we were told—and sold. One day in the summer of

1950 I picked up a paper and read "North Korea Invades South Korea!"

"Where's that?" I asked. I soon found out. A few days later we were "on alert" and that meant active duty. I found myself in California in combat training.

Being a Christian also means that we are "on alert." We are in the active reserve. There are no "associate memberships" in the church. All of Christ's followers are on active duty in his cause.

Yet, a strange attitude is seen among many of the popular dispensational authors. They actually teach against alertness, not overtly but by the force of what they are saying. The programs they have created allow them to say, "The second coming can't come yet, for the three and a half years of tribulation haven't occurred yet"; or, "The reconstituted Roman Empire is not formed yet, so the second coming is still in the future"; or again, "The Antichrist hasn't shown up yet, so it can't be the end." Unwittingly, this type of interpretation destroys the need for alertness. It really is another way of saying "We know the times and the seasons." Obviously the New Testament writers did not share in any thought system which ruled out alertness.

Alertness Means Reality

Albert Speer, minister of armaments in Nazi Germany, wrote an interesting account of the last days in Hitler's Berlin bunker. Speer says there was a "fairyland atmosphere" inside the bunker. Outside, the Russian and American armies were pounding the Third Reich into powder. Inside the bunker Hitler pored over maps and made decisions to attack with nonexistent armies and air forces. He raved of last-minute super weapons and of the allies going to war against each other. Speer found such unreality disgusting. Nothing would change Hitler's mind until the crushing march of events drove him to suicide.

The New Testament emphasis upon alertness does not permit us to live in a theological fairyland. As Paul said to the believers in Thessalonica, "When people say, 'there is peace and security,' then sudden destruction will come upon them" (1 Thess. 5:3). To be alert is to be aware of what is going on outside our bunkers. It is to live in the clear light of present duty instead of wandering in the fog of speculation.

Confident at His Coming

Christians do not await Christ as frightened rabbits await the fox. Instead, Scripture instills within us the attitude of confident hope at his coming.

Few churches have been as spiritually immature as the first century church at Corinth. Yet even to these kindergarten Christians Paul is able to write:

> You are not lacking in any spiritual gift, as you wait for the revealing of our Lord Jesus Christ; who will sustain you to the end, guiltless in the day of our Lord Jesus Christ. God is faithful, by whom you were called into the fellowship of his son, Jesus Christ our Lord.
>
> 1 Corinthians 1:7-9

Jesus will sustain, God is faithful. In other words, God wants you to know he is on your side. God wants you to make it!

For the faithful, therefore, Christ's return will

not be a frightening encounter. It is an event for which they wait with eager anticipation: "So Christ, having been offered once to bear the sins of many, will appear a second time, not to deal with sin but to save those who are eagerly waiting for him" (Heb. 9:28). This expectation, this eager longing, creates the present hope that transforms the imperfections of the present. Hope means knowing that a glorious new order will sweep away what is limiting the perfection to come. In Romans 8 Paul raises the theme of expectation to a poetic summit:

> The creation awaits with eager longing for the revealing of the sons of God . . . because the creation itself will be set free from its bondage to decay and obtain the glorious liberty of the children of God.

> Romans 8:19, 21

For every believer who has been saddened by the injustices of this life, who has been baffled at the seeming success of the wicked and the difficulties of the righteous, who has shed frustrated tears at the suffering of a child, who has stood speechless in the presence of death—for these, Christ's return means the vindication of the right, the healing of every tear, the releasing of creation from decay and death.

God Wants Us to Make It

While in the Marines, I encountered an extraordinarily tough obstacle course at Quantico, Va. This course was so hard that its name was a "cussword." While we hapless officer candidates thudded into walls and swung giddily over pits, the drill instructors called words of "encouragement": "If the twelve-foot wall doesn't get you, the ten-foot pit will!" Or, "Don't let this course kill you, let us do it!" And, "I don't think you guys have the guts to finish this thing."

Too many people look at Christianity as though it were a spiritual obstacle course. In this view, God is the Drill Instructor trying to eliminate as many people as he can. This is a strange, barbed-wire concept of the faith. Paul said to the disciples at Philippi, "I am confident of this particular thing, that he who started a good work in you will thoroughly complete it right up to the day of Christ Jesus" * (Phil. 1:6). How could Paul be so confident? Because God has done more than anyone else to ensure that we make it. He gave his Son to make it possible for us to be confident in the final hour.

It is this enormous investment that gives us confident hope. In the Bible, hope does not mean wishful thinking as in "I sure hope I make it." Hope means confident expectation. As one writer says, "Hope is faith turned toward the future." God has given us this kind of hope. It does not come from our own circumstances or ability, but from God:

Blessed be the God and Father of our Lord Jesus Christ! By his great mercy we have been born anew to a living hope through the resurrection of Jesus Christ from the dead, and to an inheritance which is imperishable, undefiled, and unfading, kept in heaven for you.

1 Peter 1:3-4

A Living Hope

Peter says we have a living hope, a hope that gives us life and joy. Some hopes are empty and futile; they will inevitably disappoint us. If we base our future on whether the stock market will go up, whether gasoline will become cheaper, whether jobs will be easier to find, we set ourselves up to be crushed. We must have something with more certainty: "Hope does not disappoint us, because God's love has been poured out in our hearts through the Holy Spirit who was given to us" (Rom. 5:5). God has pledged our hope by sharing himself with us. He wants us to make it. This is why we do "not grieve as others do who have no hope" (1 Thess. 4:13).

If we continue to abide in Christ, we will never have to "shrink from him in shame at his coming" (1 John 2:28). We will face judgment with confidence (1 John 4:16-19).

I know the world has lost hope. It is not happy nor contented. But what of the believers? Even the world's darkest hour is to be for them an hour of illumination. As Helmut Thielicke has said: "The final hour belongs to us; shall we be anxious about the next minute?" [1]

No; for Christ's return teaches us responsibility, alertness, and hope.

---

[1] Helmut Thielicke, *Christ and the Meaning of Life* (Grand Rapids, Mich.: Baker Book House, 1975), p. 137.

_6 *Winning the* Battle

The Winter Olympic Games of 1980 featured an amazing series of victories by a young, relatively inexperienced American hockey team. The team was a hasty collection of collegians put together only for this competition. Few gave them any major consideration for a decent finish, much less winning the whole thing. After all, they were facing older, far more experienced players from around the world. Among the teams they would face was the Soviet team. Now that was a hockey team! Had they not crushed even professionals? But an astounding thing happened. The youthful Americans discovered a winning spirit, and bigger, more powerful teams, began to fall. Even the previously invincible Soviets were defeated. After the gold medal was claimed, a marvelous spirit of victory surged through the nation. Daily crises faded for just a moment as the country basked warmly in the unexpected triumph. But, true to form, only a day or so later the old spirit of pessimism and strife dominated the news as before. It was a bright, brief hour, but underneath nothing had really changed.

The history of the world is filled with the stimulating power of temporary victories. The year 1945 saw two significant days in America, V-E Day and V-J Day. On those days in which victory in Europe and Japan were celebrated, respectively, America went wild. People danced in the streets, strangers embraced, grown men cried as a feeling of general euphoria suffused the country. But the cold, gray dawn of postwar realities soon chilled those shouts of triumph. The cold war with Russia and a host of other problems dashed the spirit of victory again. The impact of temporary victories is not felt very long.

The Conqueror of the World

As stimulating as sporting victories can be, as exciting as great conquests of warfare can be, they seem to have limited effects on human expectations and attitudes. Overwhelming problems create new crises in the human spirit and rob the joy of victory. A much more permanent victory than those achieved in warfare or sports is needed to give us joy. A more enduring hero than a winning sportsman is needed for long-term inspiration. Only a truly great Champion can change joyless people who live from one petty victory to another into those who know they are always eternal winners.

There is such a Victor. At one point he made the astounding claim, "I have conquered the world!" No, it was not Alexander the Great who sustained this claim, for he now lies in a forgotten Babylonian tomb. It was not Attila, nor the Caesars, nor Charlemagne, nor any military conqueror. Jesus Christ made that statement before his greatest battle—one from which he emerged as the absolute Victor: "In the world you have tribulation; but be of good cheer, I have overcome the world" (John 16:33). His greatest conquest was not over a piece of land, but over sin and death, the two most relentless enemies of human happiness. Jesus was the only one qualified to enter this struggle, and he is the only winner to emerge from that contest. His outreach to mankind is designed to share the fruits of his victory with us:

> "Now is the judgment of this world, now shall the ruler of this world be cast out; and I, when I am lifted up from the earth, will draw all men to myself." He said this to show by what death he was to die.
>
> John 12:31-33

The sovereignty of Jesus imparts the spirit of victory for all time because his victory is the only one of eternal value.

The Theme of Complete Victory

Of all the literature in the Bible, the prophetic and apocalyptic sections probably contribute most to the theme of the future joy of victory. A solid example of that appears in Revelation 1:4-6. We shall see that the book of Revelation resounds with the theme of victory in Christ.

Yet this important point is oddly neglected in much of the material being published on the last things today. Somewhere in the briar patch of schedules and agendas the true way has been lost. The great good news that Jesus is the Winner, that he was victorious through death and resurrection, has been neglected. That he promises that same victory to believers is a major theme of future-oriented passages in the Bible. Believers needed that emphasis then; we need it today.

Jesus overcame; he is victorious. First century disciples faced death (Rev. 2:10). They needed to know they would share in the victory of Jesus. They were winners because their Master was a winner, but they needed to hear this from Jesus himself. That is why John shares these thoughts from the very lips of the Lord: " 'Fear not, I am the first and the last, and the living one; I died, and behold I am alive for evermore' " (Rev. 1:17-18).

Again we see how utterly frustrating it would have been to these believers, who lived with daily threats to their livelihood and lives, if John had said: "The revelation I received from the Lord is about what will happen thousands of years in the future. The people of that time will have some great things happen in their era. Some of the Christians then will be 'raptured' away secretly." What a zero this would be in terms of strengthening the church of that time. The Lord proceeds on a tack opposite to the speculative approach. He meets the problems of Christians at that time with affirmation that victory is in the Lamb—then and there!

And I heard a loud voice in heaven saying, "Now the salvation and the power and the kingdom of our God and the authority of his Christ have come, for the accuser of our brethren has been thrown down, who accuses them day and night before our God. And they have conquered him by the blood of the Lamb and by the word of their testimony, for they loved not their lives even unto death."
Revelation 12:10-11

Christians of every era take comfort in these affirmations, but the primary application began in John's time. The complete victory is for all believers.

The Conquerors

Jesus definitely intends for his followers to know they are winners in him. This is such a strongly stressed theme in the book of Revelation that surprisingly it is only lightly spoken of in contemporary presentations. This book repeats a series of blessings to those who conquer through the strength of Jesus. The status of a conqueror is not static but dynamic, for the original language consistently uses a present participle, *ho nikōn,* "he who conquers." Conquering is an ongoing process which derives from the atoning blood of the Lamb (Rev. 12:11). Here are Jesus' promises to those conquering in him:

(1) They will have access to the tree of life (Rev. 2:7). As access to life was cut off in Adam and Eve, so it is restored in Christ.

(2) They will not be harmed by the second death (Rev. 2:11). The first death is physical, the second spiritual. It is to suffer "the punishment of eternal destruction and exclusion from the presence of the Lord" (2 Thess. 1:9).

(3) They will have the secret manna and the white stone of approval (Rev. 2:17). The secret manna is the "bread of life" mentioned in John 6:33-35. It is a source of strength to which the world is stranger. The white stone was used as a YES ballot in voting. It stands for the fact that the conqueror in Christ is sustained and approved by God.

(4) They will triumph over the pagans and receive the morning star (Rev. 2:26-28). Pagan lifestyles will not win out. The true victors will be from the class of those who put God ahead of hedonistic pursuits. The morning star is another name for Jesus (Rev. 22:16).

(5) They will receive the symbolic clothing of white and will be entered in the Book of Life (Rev. 3:5). White clothing stands for the righteousness which God bestows on those who trust in him (Rev. 7:14). By God's graciousness they are entered into life sustained by the victory of the Lamb.

(6) They will be an immovable pillar in God's sanctuary (Rev. 3:12). This has to do with stability and certainty. God will see that his winning people are never has-beens.

(7) They will share Christ's authority in the presence of the Father (Rev. 3:21). Winners reign along with Christ; they are never second class.

(8) They will inherit all the newness of the ultimate age (Rev. 21:1, 7). All things fresh, lovely, and permanent belong to those who are victorious in Christ. Their victory is as morning dew, fresh throughout all the ages. The joy of winning is eternally theirs.

Thus Jesus revealed to John that those conquering by the blood of the Lamb will have an eternal victory—a victory that means life, no separation from God, sustenance and approval from God, vindication in choosing Jesus, forgiveness, permanent stability, sharing in great authority, and eternal freshness of joy.

We have all seen those contests where they say, "Everybody's a winner." In Jesus that is true. You may be a loser in every contest you enter, but in Jesus you are a winner because Jesus is a Winner. That theme is central to what the Bible says about the end of all things: *God's people are going to win!*

But, in the meantime, we do have a war on our hands.

The Christian Warfare

The symbolism of Revelation is often militaristic. This is to remind us we have a war on our hands. We are all called on to be "good soldiers of Christ Jesus" (2 Tim. 2:3). While we are at war, we are not using destructive weapons on people or real estate. There are no such things as Christian storm troopers. We are not fighting people, we are fighting evil forces (Eph. 6:12), evil influences, evil life-styles. We are not to be like the infamous Friar Torquemada of the Spanish Inquisition who had heretics burned at the stake. We want only to expose people to the warmth of God's love. Paul tells us of our real weapons:

> For though we live in the world we are not carrying on a worldly war, for the weapons of our warfare are not worldly but have divine power to destroy strongholds. We destroy arguments and every proud obstacle to the knowledge of God, and take every thought captive to obey Christ.

> 2 Corinthians 10:3-5

Christ's Word furnishes the power we need. Christ's Spirit sustains us in the struggle. We need not resort to devious and unwholesome tactics (2 Cor. 4:1ff.). We must keep our spirit of victory honestly as we struggle in our victorious cause right on up to the complete culmination of Christ's victory. An ugly spirit is a mark that we still share the attitude of the world (1 John 4:7-8).

D-Day and V-Day

The German scholar Oscar Cullman once remarked that Christians live between "D-Day" and "V-Day." By this he meant that in Christ's resurrection the decisive spiritual battle has been fought, as the Allies invasion of Normandy—World War II's D-Day—signaled the inevitable defeat of Germany. But as V-Day was yet to come, there still remains, in our spiritual struggle, the mopping-up action and the deliverance of all those still under the enemy's power. Victory is assured; it is only a matter of time.

Something very like this is depicted in the book of Revelation. In chapter 12 the devil suffers a stunning, crushing defeat in his warfare in the heavenly spheres (12:7ff.). This defeat occurs in the context of the birth and subsequent ascension of Christ (12:4-6). Satan then launches a bitter campaign against those whom he can reach, pulling in allies from world empires (the monster of Revelation 13 who comes from the sea). He also enlists false religious ideas as an ally (the lamb-like monster of 13:11ff.). In spite of all this help, Satan and his allies go down to ultimate defeat (Rev. 18–20). The point of John's analysis is that even though Satan is a defeated enemy, he is still dangerous. Like a wounded monster he still has power to hurt with terrible force those who come into his grasp. D-Day does not mean we can relax. It is a call to be vigilant to the final hour.

Armageddon

The mysterious battle of Armageddon is probably another variation on the same theme of the decisive defeat of evil. Armageddon is Hebrew for "mountain of Megiddo." Megiddo, however, is not a mountain but a plain. The nearest mountain is Mount Carmel. Megiddo was an ancient battlefield. Josiah, the reforming king of Judah, was slain here, and other important battles were fought at Megiddo. It would be like saying "Gettysburg" or "Waterloo," for the only important thing which had ever happened there was a battle.

But what about the word "mountain"? It is possible John is combining two ideas here—the idea of a decisive battle and the famous description by Jeremiah of Babylon as a "destroying mountain" (Jer. 51:25). This is quite likely since the immediate context around the mention of Armageddon in Revelation 16 has to do with the Babylon of that day (Rome). Verses 17-19 deal with the defeat of Babylon, the great city which allied itself with Satan against God's people. Thus John would be saying that evil will suffer a decisive defeat. Notice how strongly this comes across in Jeremiah:

> Behold, I am against you,
> O destroying mountain,
>   says the Lord,
> which destroys the whole earth;
> I will stretch out my hand against
>   you,
> and roll you down from the
>   crags,
> and make you a burnt mountain.

Jeremiah 51:25

John's readers would certainly get the point, and remembering how God had indeed caused the destruction of ancient Babylon, they would see the handwriting on the wall against Rome, the "Babylon" of that day. Thus this symbol becomes a reminder that evil suffers a crushing defeat. It has met its "Waterloo" so to speak. Satan, the destroying mountain, has met its Megiddo! Thus the enemies of God face their appointment with Armageddon. Evil has had its D-Day, but Christ's people carry on the struggle right on up to V-Day.

No Substitute for Victory

General Douglas MacArthur said upon being forbidden to pursue the enemy into their sanctuaries: "In warfare there is no substitute for victory." This is also true of our spiritual warfare. Since the decisive battle has been won by Christ, no one needs to lose this struggle But since the mopping-up operations still face us, we must struggle faithfully in the spirit of his victory. We need not be like a downhearted believer who found himself in prison for his faith and wrote these lines: "Is there something in me like a beaten army, fleeing from a victory already won?"

We must be alert to those defeatist elements in us which seek to deny us the fruits of the victory already achieved by Christ. To this end the theme of the Bible's prophetic and apocalyptic literature replies: "They have conquered . . . by the blood of the Lamb and by the word of their testimony" (Rev. 12:11).

7 Defeating Death

Death is not the last thing. It is the last enemy (1 Cor. 15:26). The theme of 1 Corinthians 15 is the defeat of this enemy. There are no human solutions to the problem of death. Through the ages mankind has been counseled to be philosophical about it, or, to "rage, rage against the dying of the light," as Dylan Thomas suggests in his "Do Not Go Gentle into That Good Night." Still, the only real answer to the problem of death is the Christian answer.

Yet, a great deal of future-oriented writing neglects this answer. Much of the biblical material on the end times is treated speculatively instead of being practically applied to the problem of death. Sometimes it is forgotten that this type of writing was ultimately designed to be faith-strengthening good news of victory over persecution and death. As Paul says so well:

> But in fact Christ has been raised from the dead, the first fruits of those who have fallen asleep. For as by a man came death, by a man has come also the resurrection of the

dead. For as in Adam all die, so also in Christ shall all be made alive.

1 Corinthians 15:20-23

Death and Our Future

How can we speak of death and a future in the same breath? From a human point of view the two exclude each other. But the Bible offers more than a human point of view. We have the spectacle of God beating death back into a place of ineffectiveness: "Then Death and Hades were thrown into the lake of fire" (Rev. 20:14). The key to this victory over death is Jesus Christ. What God did in Christ has assured believers of the defeat of this last enemy. When Christ was raised, "Death had to let his prize possession go free."[1] We obtained our freedom in that action of God and thus are assured of a future where death is not the final event.

A Common Foe

Many people in the ancient world groaned in fear of death. Many of the inscriptions on pagan tombs are loud protests against the fates which bring death. Believers in the first century lived in a time obsessed with death and the fear of death. Alexander the Great is said to have had a model of a skeleton placed before him at every meal.

Believers in John's time depended on his great vision of Christ in the Revelation to let them know that death could not rob them of their future with God. Jesus' appearance to John in Revelation 1 sets the tone of much that follows. The words of Jesus to John, "Fear not," are precisely what John and the church needed to hear. Fear was their greatest enemy at this point, especially fear of death. But Jesus promises, "Be faithful unto death, and I will give you the crown of life" (Rev. 2:10); and "He who conquers shall not be hurt by the second death" (2:11). This is why the angel can relay to believers the message, "Blessed are the dead who die in the Lord henceforth" (14:13).

The Fear Continues

Believers in our age also live in a culture obsessed with the fear of death. Gail Sheehy underscores this fear in a section from her best-selling work, *Passages*. She talks of an experience she had in Northern Ireland when a man was shot to death in her presence. The death of this man was shocking, but it did not turn out to be the real trauma. Something more dreadful emerged:

> Real bullets had threatened my life from the outside. It was an observable event. My fears were appropriate. Now the destructive force was inside me. I was my own event. I could not escape it. Something alien, horrible, unspeakable, but undeniable, had begun to inhabit me. My own death.[2]

"My own death." Few words are more sobering to modern man. Supposedly liberated people can be quite glib about formerly fearsome topics such as sex, but they pale at the thought of their death. A modern philosopher has said: "Death is an iron ring around life." It is the chilling silencer of otherwise loquacious commentators. Believers face the double challenge of not being infected by this virus of fear and being able to share the cure with a fearful world.

You Only Live Forever!

"You only go around once." So the guy in the beer commercial you-knowed at us for the one millionth time. I could have shouted back: "You only live forever, you know!" But, maybe he didn't know; so few do.

To the dispirited worldling the Christian has one heartening affirmation: The gospel is a message of life! Paul makes it clear in his second letter to Timothy that Jesus came to do more than pass on a few noteworthy thoughts. He speaks of "Our Savior Christ Jesus, who abolished death and brought life and immortality to light through the gospel" (2 Tim. 1:10). Jesus came to put death out of business.

John is assured of the same thing by Jesus himself: "Fear not, I am the first and the last, and the living one; I died, and behold I am alive for evermore, and I have the keys of Death and Hades" (Rev. 1:17-18). This saying must have startled John and his fellow believers. Did Jesus have the keys of life and death? All along it had seemed as if Caesar or some provincial proconsul did. But Jesus is only repeating to John what he had earlier said to Pilate, who had asked:

> "Do you not know that I have power to release you, and power to crucify you?" Jesus answered him, "You would have no power over me unless it had been given you from above."
>
> John 19:10-11

"The keys," Jesus is saying, "are in my hands, not yours."

While most believers today are fortunately not

faced with the threat of death from persecutors, they still need to hear and share in Jesus' victory over death. One reason we have seen already is that we live in a death-evading culture. We may be infected with the fear of death from the world and tempted to deny the reality of death altogether. Or we may engage in fits of depression because we are physically perishable. Death is one of those events we should not attempt to deny, because it compels us to face the ultimate priorities of life. Yet we should not fear the perishing of the body, for only then can we put on the new and immortal body Jesus has prepared for us (1 Cor. 15:35ff.).

In asserting that he holds the keys to death, as in Revelation 1:17-18, Jesus faces the question of death head on. He not only has obtained authority over death, he has experienced it and triumphed over it—"I died," he plainly says. But beyond this, he lives forevermore. Contrast this experience with those holding unbiblical theories about death and what follows death. The difference is between One who speaks from personal encounter, and those who are merely guessing.

The Meaning of the Keys

To have a key is to have control over something otherwise locked to us. To entrust our death to Christ, who has the key to death, is to gain control over this ancient enemy. Other "keys" fail. Marxism, with its depreciation of the individual, explains death as an economic necessity. The older members of the herd must go under so that the younger may ascend. Atheistic thinkers such as Albert Camus and Jean Paul Sartre say death is simply absurd. Macho street philosophy glorifies living on the edge; if death comes, at least you lived life to the fullest. All such views are false keys. They admit us to no control over death.

A key also stands for a solution to or understanding of a problem. Jesus not only has control over death, he also comprehends it. The experience of death which gave Jesus mastery over it has now been placed at his disciples' disposal (Heb. 2:14-15). God places Jesus' experience at my disposal that I might conquer my fear of death.

Guidance through Death

In the next chapter on what happens *after* death, we will notice there are plenty of would-be guides. The same thing is true of those who believe they know what happens *at* death. Yet, we have no one with the integrity of Jesus who has gone through this experience and come back to report on it. When it comes to the matter of death we must have a reliable guide with genuine credentials. Aristophanes' play, *Frogs,* has a humorous theme about two travelers to Hades, Dionysius and his servant Xanthius. These two characters blunder all over the Greek underworld in a comedy of misguided effort. Perhaps even Aristophanes recognized there were no real guides to death. Of course the Greek author was not privileged to have heard of Christ, who says to his servants that he has been where no traveler has ever gone and returned. And, praise God, he has returned!

Jesus prepares us in part for experiencing death by the experience of conversion. In our conversion to him we have already shared, in one sense, in his death and resurrection. Our burial with him in baptism was a likeness of his death; and our emerging to live the Christian life is a sharing in his resurrection (Rom. 6:1ff.). If this does not seem radical enough to prepare us for death, we are not taking conversion seriously enough. For nothing can be more radical than becoming a believer in Christ. Richard Wolff, the German scholar, underscores this truth:

> The Christian is far better equipped than most to confront radical change, even the final experience of total transformation. The Christian has already welcomed the most extreme transition, turning toward God.[3]

Our encounter with the transforming power of Jesus in conversion is an excellent beginning for change, even the change of death.

Death as Gain

What is the meaning of death for the Christian? Would you imagine the word "gain" could be used in the same context with death? Paul does so:

> For to me being alive means Christ and to die is gain. Now if I live on in a physical life, it will mean fruitful work for me, and which I should choose I do not know. I am pulled both ways, since I long to depart and be with Christ, which is certainly better in every way; but to continue physical life is of greater necessity for your benefit.[*]

Philippians 1:21-23

Paul expresses the tension he feels between remaining in a useful ministry on earth and departing for Christ. He has no trace of morbidity, no pensiveness, not even faint sadness. Instead Paul speaks of death as "gain." He can say this because for him dying meant *more of Christ!* It is gain not

78

because of some golden mansion coveted by a materialistic heart, but because Christ is the reward.

Someone has suggested that this passage can best be understood as an equation: "For me to live means X; for me to die means Y." If anything other than Christ appears where X is, it is impossible for Y to appear as "gain." Try it:

For me to live means *$$$$$;* to die is *losing it all.*

For me to live means *power;* to die is *losing control.*

For me to live means *pleasure;* to die means *deprivation.*

Try any combination and it always comes out the same. Unless living means Jesus Christ for you, death cannot mean gain.

Jesus Affirms Life

Yet, for all his willingness to depart and be with Christ, Paul was ready to continue to live on earth. Although Jesus prepares us for death, he may ask us to live. We must accept his call to continue our ministry in this life, if that is his desire. Sometimes it takes more courage to live for Christ than to die for him. Jesus affirms life, whether here or hereafter. Even death is only a means to life. It is not death that is sought, but life.

Sometimes believers can become intoxicated with the idea of dying for Christ. This can lead to a kamikaze-type religion. The second century Christian leader Ignatius left a letter called *To the Romans* in which he says:

I would enjoy the wild beasts prepared for me and I pray they may be ready for me; I will flatter these beasts to devour me quickly, not

79

acting as they did toward some they feared to touch. And if they prove unwilling, I will compel them to do it (author's translation).

The courage expressed is commendable, but it is love, not courage, that defeats death. If God wills for us to live on, let us accept Jesus' affirmation of life.

Tents Aren't Made to Last Forever

Jesus' victory over death gives us more than a future hope. It also gives us confident life in the here and now. Accepting his triumph allows us solidarity with Christ in both life and death. It is "eternal life," beginning now and extending into the future. As John says, "This is the testimony, that God gave us eternal life, and this life is in his Son. He who has the Son has life; he who has not the Son of God has not life" (1 John 5:11-12).

When you were small, what a thrill it was to camp out bravely in the backyard. It was a great adventure; you shivered awhile and got good and wet. All along you were sustained by knowing that warm solid house was there and inside were people who cared about you. And sometime in the middle of the night you may have left your tent and gone into the house. It was more solid and secure. And "We know that if the earthly tent we live in is destroyed, we have a building from God, a house not made with hands, eternal in the heavens" (2 Cor. 5:1). Tents weren't made to last forever, but life was!

---

[1]J. Verkuyl, *The Message of Liberation in Our Age* (Grand Rapids, Mich.: Eerdmans Publishing Company, 1970), p. 61.

[2]Gail Sheehy, *Passages* (New York: Bantam Books, 1977) p. 11.

[3]Richard Wolff, *The Last Enemy* (Washington, D.C.: Canon Press, 1974), p. 56.

8 Facing the Unknown

My father died when I was four years old. Little remains in my memory of him. Snatches of impressions are there. A figure sits at the table, hearty, laughing. Then he is sick in bed, then . . . a blank. I thought little about his death until I was about eleven. One summer day while out hiking to the edge of town with some friends, we came near the cemetery where my father was buried. I decided to look for his grave. I had never seen it, since I had not gone to the funeral. It was a silly thing, or did I have some need to know he was really dead, and not just . . . ? What? I didn't know, but the grave would prove it. By then it was nearly dusk. I ran from corner to corner of the cemetery, peering at gravestone after gravestone, looking for the familiar name, the same as my own, but I could not find it. Then it was dark, and I headed home, my search unsuccessful. A feeling began to surface within me, alien and dreadful, a feeling I had not experienced before: "What of death? And what happens *after* death?" This question brought on a sense of hopelessness and depression.

My mother met me, and, instead of lecturing me on being late, she listened thoughtfully to my story. How grateful I am for her attention and kindness that night! She tried to explain about death, but I never really understood the answer until I became a Christian. That was many years afterward. The answer was—Christ. There was One with us during that hour and *afterward* also. Fear and dread could be handled, because death and the unseen were in his hands.

The Keys of the Unseen World

We have dwelt extensively on the passage in the first chapter of Revelation, where Jesus speaks to the frightened John, because it is central to our hope. It has even more to teach us. Jesus said to John and other believers who face death and the unknown: "I have the keys to Death and Hades . . . ." Jesus affirms that he is still in control at death, and after death. This is precisely what suffering Christians needed to hear in John's time. It is also what we need to hear in this present time. The prophetic element deals again with real needs of real people.

Before we can see clearly the map which Jesus has prepared for all who wish insight into the unseen, some definitions are in order. "Hades" is a transliteration of the Greek word *haides*. It is a mistake to translate this word "hell," as do some English versions. Hades refers to the unseen world of the dead, while hell is the part of that realm reserved for the wicked. Hades is from the word used in the Greek Old Testament to render the Hebrew word *sheol*. *Sheol* means "the grave" or "the realm of the dead" (cf. Job 10:21; 38:17; Isa. 14:9). In the New Testament, Hades refers to the realm of the dead, whether righteous (Acts 2:27) or wicked (Luke 16:23). It also refers to powers in the unseen world conceived to be in opposition to God's purposes (as in Matt. 16:18).

Jesus the Key-Holder

Jesus, who experienced an encounter with the realm of the dead, was not abandoned in Hades but was raised by God (Acts 2:31). Thus Jesus can tell John that He has control over this realm as well as over the malignant evil powers. Jesus alone has the key to the truth about these realms. In John's day many claimed to have insight into the unseen world; and it is no different today. Various claimants exist who purport to have insight into what follows this earthly life. Can their maps be true, or are they misshapen products of human imagination?

Not long ago in our city a car dealer sponsored a sales promotion. He distributed thousands of keys to a "treasure chest" on display at his dealership. The idea was to come in and try your key on the chest. Of course, while there, a big try was made to get you to buy an automobile. One or two real keys existed; everybody else had a blank. A great many people ended up with keys that would open absolutely nothing. We lost nothing big, only a little time. But what about trusting in a blank key to unlock something really important? What if the key we have been given by somebody to unlock the truth about death and the afterlife is a phony? That's serious. A useless key here would be tragic.

Life After Life?

Jesus' view of life after life is one thing, but Dr. Raymond Moody, Jr.'s is another. Dr. Moody and his predecessor, Dr. Elisabeth Kubler-Ross, claim to have discovered an important key to life after death. His book, *Life After Life,* details the analysis of what may happen when one dies. In the process, wittingly or not, he affirms another key to the world beyond.

Dr. Moody bases his viewpoint upon certain experiences related by persons who were clinically "dead" but who were subsequently revived. Dr. Moody makes a systematic analysis of the components of these experiences. He describes various phenomena reported, such as a sensation of free-floating over the body, flying through some sort of tunnel of darkness, and meeting a "being of light" who communicates in some way with the person involved. Those interviewed did not agree on the details, but Moody claims much correspondence. Also discovered were persons who described unpleasant experiences, sometimes dreadful and frightening. All these experiences seemed to have little correlation with a person's belief system, although Moody has spent little time on this point.

The effect of this "research" seems to be that, without too many exceptions, most people can look forward to a fairly pleasant if somewhat vague experience upon dying. Previous preparation for death seems to have little bearing; at least Moody does not consider it important enough to mention. If any attitude is encouraged by this approach it would seem to be a certain passivity toward death and the afterlife.

Are these trustworthy keys? A look at the specific biblical answer to this will be made later. First, let us look at a critique suggested by Rusty Wright, a Crusade for Christ staff member. Wright has stated certain objections to Moody's view in his book *The Other Side of Life*. Wright suggests several possible explanations of the experiences Moody describes:

(1) They may be physiological effects of such things as oxygen deficiency, brain pressure, blood factors, etc.

(2) They may be chemical or drug-related in nature, perhaps induced by anesthesia or allergic reactions.

(3) The experiences could be Satan-inspired to delude unprepared persons into not preparing for death.

(4) They may be God-inspired to encourage frightened Christians.

Perhaps the first two of these explanations are possible. The last two suggestions I find about as subjective as Moody's interpretations. If a person is at the point of death anyway, and he is unprepared, Satan has nothing to gain by deluding him further. He's already done an adequate job. And, as for the Christian, he already has *every* possible assurance against fearing death.

As Dead as Jesus?

The biggest question, from an objective viewpoint, is: Were any of these persons *dead?* This simply cannot be answered by the criteria available today. Even the Harvard standards for determining death are still under question in the courts of the land. Just because Dr. Moody and others considered such persons as "dead" enough to have a valid experience is begging the question. In fact, they were all "alive" when they related their experience. So much remains to be discovered about physical death that it would be perilous to assume anything from these studies.

Jesus is a better guide to the unseen world after death because, unlike the subjects in the Moody interviews, he really died! "I died" is his statement to John in Revelation 1:18. We know that among the witnesses to Jesus' death were hardened Romans who had seen many deaths. They would not be fooled (John 19:33). Besides Jesus lived in a time where the techniques of medical revival of life were unknown. Jesus died. But he did not remain in the realm of the dead. Years before the death of Jesus, the Psalmist had predicted he would not remain in Hades but would be raised from death (Ps. 16:8-11; Acts 2:31). The "experiences" related by Dr. Moody cannot be reliable guidelines, for death did not really occur. We need a guide who has actually been dead, not someone assumed to have been.

Jesus is that experienced guide. In fact, the writer of Hebrews uses precisely that term to describe him. He says Jesus is our *prodromos* (Heb. 6:20). The *prodromos* was a guide who explored enemy territory before the main body of the army went into the land. Jesus has scouted the territory ahead for us. Better to rely on one experienced guide than a trainload of greenhorns.

Reincarnation—Another Blank Key?

Another popular "key" to the afterlife, the doctrine of reincarnation, is appearing regularly in America today as Eastern religions become more widespread. Edgar Cayce's understanding of the afterlife and other schools of thought also support the theory of multiple lives for one "soul." This idea, an ancient one going back at least to the Hindu *Vedas,* encourages the believer in the system to use his present life to prepare for a better existence the next time around. As explained by the Hindu devotee Damodara Dasa:

> The vast wheel of birth and death carries the soul on its seemingly endless sojourn through 8,400,000 species of life. . . . Our next body after this one is better or worse according to the quality of our activities in this life. If we're saintly, we'll get a saintly body next time, but if we're doggish, we'd better prepare for a dog's life after this one. This is the law of *karma* . . . . So the millionaire and the genius are reaping the benefits of good karma, and the pauper and the dunce, having committed sinful activities, are getting their just deserts . . . .

Of course, this is strongly colored with human-centered merit, but the doctrine, at least as suggested above, has profound social implications. The teaching of reincarnation is undoubtedly a cry of protest against the social injustice of the Hindu caste system. But there are grave spiritual objections to this position.

Why Jesus Is a Better Guide

Jesus is a better guide to the realities that exist after this life than the Hindu sages. Jesus' story of the rich man and Lazarus (Luke 16:19-31) was meant to encourage responsible living, not to provide a topographical tour of the realm of the dead. The story contains ideas current in Jewish thought of Jesus' time. Was Jesus accurately describing Hades, or merely building on the concepts of his audience? It is probably impossible to know if this story is a valid description of the minute details of the Hadean world.

However, it does give some general principles about what happens after death. First, people do not return from Hades to this present world, which counters Moody's deathbed testimonials and the theory of reincarnation. Second, people in Hades still maintain their personal identities. They do not return to earth in another form of life, nor are they absorbed into a general "world soul." Third, there is no second chance in Hades—people's destinies are fixed at death. Fourth, the afterlife is a pleasant experience for the righteous. Fifth, those who neglect God's people are punished in Hades.

Jesus also attacked the social ideas implicit in reincarnation even though he never attacked reincarnation per se. The man born blind in John 9 is not blind because of his sin nor his parent's sin (John 9:1ff.). He can be helped—in fact, he should be helped—because it is a work of God to help him. Reincarnation teaches that if we are miserable we deserve it; in fact, we deserve to be whatever we are. This is a locked-in system in which it becomes a crime to try to help someone. People who affirm reincarnation are painting themselves into a fatalistic corner with no hope. But this view of life after life is no key at all, for as Scripture plainly says: "It is appointed to men to die once, and after that comes judgment" (Heb. 9:27). Not many deaths, many cycles, but death, then God. Thus these "keys" to life after death are shown to be both inadequate and false. The key to a pleasant death is not passivity but knowing Jesus. The key to a better life after death is not in striving to earn enough credit to exist on a higher plane in another life, but in letting Jesus transform our one and only existence into a life of eternal value.

The Powers of the Unseen World

Instead of going randomly into death, merely passive or actively deluded, we must put ourselves into the hands of the One who can deal with what happens *after*. But even *before* death malignant powers exist who would like to subvert the joy of our present life. Our present struggle, Paul reminds us, is not "against flesh and blood, but against the principalities, against the powers, against the world rulers of this present darkness, against the spiritual hosts of wickedness in the heavenly places" (Eph. 6:12).

Jesus says there is one relationship which even the powers of the unseen world cannot resist. This is the relationship with Father, Son, and Holy Spirit in the church: "I will build my church, and the powers of death shall not prevail against it" (Matt. 16:18). The word translated "death" is literally *Hades*, the unseen world. This control over unseen powers is probably behind the difficult thought expressed in 1 Peter 3:18-20:

> For Christ also died for sins once for all, the righteous for the unrighteous, that he might bring us to God, being put to death in the flesh but made alive in the spirit; in which he went and preached to the spirits in prison,

who formerly did not obey, when God's patience waited in the days of Noah, during the building of the ark, in which a few, that is, eight persons, were saved through water.

The phrase "in which he went" does not refer to "in the spirit" for this particular adverbial dative is never used this way in the New Testament. Rather the meaning is that Christ "in the state of living a spiritual life" went to the spirits in prison. When did this occur? Not necessarily between his death and resurrection, but possibly then. In any event, it was a triumphal visit.

The purpose of this mission was not to preach a "second chance" to anyone, for the spirits here are no doubt the disobedient angels referred to in Jude 6. They are mentioned as being imprisoned by God. The word "preached" is not the word for "preaching the gospel" but the word which means "to herald" or "to proclaim." Peter's point is that Jesus proclaimed to disobedient powers his victory over death. The thrust of the passage is the supremacy of Christ over death and those beings who allied themselves with the power of death. Thus Jesus has absolute control over the hostile forces which would use death to intimidate believers.

Christ unmasks some of these demonic powers in the book of Revelation. The dragon (the devil) enlists the power of the godless world empire to use economic power against Christians (Rev. 13:7ff.). False religious power which subverts the faith of many into supporting the world empire (in Revelation represented by the Roman empire, Rev. 17:17-18), is another force which contends against believers. All these powers fail. Revelation

18–20 describes the defeat of every power opposed to Christ and his people. Even death and Hades perish forever (Rev. 20:14). All powers hostile to those in Christ are nullified and swept away.

Christ—Before and After

In retrospect, the Bible affirms that Christ has the keys to death and the unseen. We are not senseless victims of death who must passively go into whatever may be beyond. The exalted guesses of the pseudo-scientific do not frighten us, nor do the religious guesses of those advocating a senseless, ceaseless round of existence. It does not matter that the Bible does not give specific details on what happens after death. In Christ the *after* is robbed of terror and uncertainty. In Christ the *before* is joyous because all the unseen powers are unable to shake our hope in God or our confidence in being with him after death. Christ gives us real life both before *and* after!

[1]_____ , *Back to the Godhead,* Vol. 11, No. 1, pp. 10-13.

9 *Awaiting the* Second Coming

Perhaps nothing excites religious curiosity more than the return of Christ. Discussing it today seems to put one into the camp of the eccentrics. Yet it is a legitimate Bible topic. The cry of the early church was often the Aramaic word "Maranatha!" ("Oh Lord, come!" 1 Cor. 16:22). While the consciousness of early Christians was on the Lord's return, they also knew Jesus had uttered one of his sternest warnings in this area. "Watch out lest anyone deceive you" is how Jesus opens a long discourse which includes this topic, recorded in Matthew 24, Mark 13, and Luke 21.

No right orientation to the problems surrounding the return of Christ can be achieved without reference to Jesus' discourse on the Mount of Olives. Since Matthew 24 is the fullest of these accounts, this discussion will confine itself to that chapter. From Jesus' discourse we should be able to see the special dimension Christ's final return has for all mankind.

A fundamental consideration at the outset is to realize that Jesus describes two events in this discourse, not one. First, he discusses the destruction of Jerusalem and its temple. Then he takes up his own return. The disciples had asked him this double question (24:3). Notice the two parts:

(1) "Tell us, when will this [destruction of temple] be?"

(2) "What will be the sign of your coming and the close of the age?"

How much of these two events did the disciples understand? Very little, no doubt, but Jesus still replies in a way that distinguishes the two questions clearly. This is important, because the two events call for two different responses. The first was largely discernible through certain obvious signs; the second is far more elusive. Present-day interpreters often confuse the two events and cause people to look for signs of Christ's return that actually referred to the destruction of Jerusalem.

The Key Verse

The key verse in the entire discourse is 24:34: "Truly, I say to you, this generation will not pass away till all these things take place."[1] Jesus must have intended this saying to be taken literally, for it only makes sense that way. This means that everything described *before* this saying must relate to events during the lifetime of that generation, and everything *after* the saying to more remote events.

The destruction of Jerusalem is a devastating example of the judgment of God on the disobedient, but it is not the final judgment. That is discussed in Matthew 25. Many events in the destruction of Jerusalem forecast the final judgment. Even so, we can avoid confusion if we stick by Jesus' key in verse 34 and apply preceding events to the lifetime of those he addressed.

Some verses in 24:1-35 may be perplexing. They seem to suggest much more than the destruction of the Jerusalem of that day. Yet, Jesus affirms that the events leading to the destruction of the city will occur in history, not at the end of history. "Wars and rumors of war" will abound; famines will occur. Still "the end is not yet" (24:6). The real key to the destructive event is pointed to in 24:15 where "the abomination that causes desolation" (NIV) of Daniel 12:11 is the sign for a general escape to the mountains.

Two things help us see that this is a local judgment on Jerusalem: (1) Daniel 12:11 connects the "sacrilege" with the taking away of the "continual burnt offering." This occurred when the Roman general Titus destroyed the temple in A.D. 70. (2) Only the inhabitants of Judea are warned to flee.

Prophetic Language

The language of 24:29ff. suggests a universal, cosmic disintegration to some, but not if we are familiar with the imagery of prophetic literature. Isaiah, for example, speaks of a day when "the stars of the heavens and their constellations will not give their light; the sun will be dark at its rising and the moon will not shed its light" (Isa. 13:10). The event? The destruction of the ancient city of Babylon. The prophets saw all creation joining in God's rebuke of sinful people. Ezekiel writes, "When I blot you out, I will cover the heavens, and make their stars dark; I will cover the sun with a cloud, and the moon shall not give its light" (Ezek. 32:7). This is a passage about the condemnation of Egypt (Ezek. 32:2), not the end of the world. So it is not surprising to find such imagery in Matthew 24, since the far more significant destruction of Jerusalem is predicted.

But what of the "Son of man coming on the clouds" (vs. 30)? Is this not more than the destruction of Jerusalem? Indeed it is, but by Jesus' own limitation it must refer to something which happened within the life span of his contemporary earthly generation. In fact, this is a direct application of Daniel's prediction of the Messiah's assumption of sovereignty:

> I saw in the night visions, and behold with the clouds of heaven there came one like a son of man, and he came to the Ancient of Days and was presented before him. And to him was given dominion and glory and kingdom, that all peoples, nations, and languages should serve him; his dominion is an everlasting dominion, which shall not pass away, and his kingdom one that shall not be destroyed.
>
> Daniel 7:13-14

"The Son of man coming on the clouds" refers to Jesus becoming Sovereign Lord, Head of God's redeemed people. This has the profoundest connection not with the end of the world but with the rejection of the Jewish state, which comes to precise fulfillment at the destruction of Jerusalem. Peter confirmed it to the house of Israel on Pentecost: "Let all the house of Israel therefore know assuredly that God has made him both Lord and Christ, this Jesus whom you crucified" (Acts 2:36). The destruction of Jerusalem was also the vindication of the Son of man (see Luke 22:69).

The Second Event

The nature of the discourse changes in 24:36. Unlike Jerusalem's destruction, no obvious warnings of Christ's return can be given. No longer are all the events to occur during the lifetime of Jesus' hearers. The date is an enigma, a mystery unknown to all except the Father. The Son had known he would be vindicated at the downfall of the Jewish state, but he did not know the date of this final event. Jesus could point to the obvious signs of the first event, but now a different note is struck.

The Day now referred to requires a decision to be vigilant, responsible, and compassionate, according to the latter verses of Matthew 24 and 25. The second coming requires absolute accountability of all nations (Matt. 25:31-33). Here again we see that the major thrust of New Testament teaching on the second coming deals with *attitudes*, not speculation. The promise of Christ's return should prompt victorious and responsible lives. Searching for signs may have been appropriate to the destruction of Jerusalem, but something far greater is expected of us as we await the final return of Jesus.

Two Appearances, One Purpose

The final return of Jesus is connected with his initial appearance on the earth. The two appearances are part of one whole. The first appearance provided the one, absolute remedy for mankind's greatest problem, alienation from God by reason of sin. The second appearance points to the total completion of Jesus' redemptive work: "So Christ, having been offered once to bear the sins of many, will appear a second time, not to deal with sin but to save those who are eagerly waiting for him" (Heb. 9:28). The early Christians looked to Christ's second appearance as the culmination of his great salvation work, not as the inauguration of a complicated, earthbound program.

Thus, Bible writers blend Christ's first appearance, the incarnation, with his second. Both direct us toward a godly life of hope:

> For the grace of God has appeared for the salvation of all men, training us to renounce irreligion and worldly passions, and to live sober, upright, and godly lives in this world, awaiting our blessed hope, the appearing of the glory of our great God and Savior Jesus Christ, who gave himself for us to redeem us from all iniquity and to purify for himself a people of his own who are zealous for good deeds.
>
> Titus 2:11-14

Unlike some premillennial views, the Bible does not teach that the second appearance of Christ is for the purpose of offering earthly domains to anyone. Houses and lands are offered to Christians *in this life,* not the future life:

> There is no man who has left house or wife or brothers or parents or children, for the sake of the kingdom of God, who will not receive manifold more in this time, and in the age to come eternal life.
>
> Luke 18:29-30

By this, Jesus no doubt means that believers inherit rich relationships in the family of God, and share their blessings with fellow believers. But it is the "age to come," beginning at the second appearance of Christ, when eternal life comes to full fruition. Yet both appearances yield a simple result—redemption, not time-setting schemes.

How Long, Lord?

Since the Lord's return is so desirable as the culmination to all that salvation promises, why has he not returned? This question baffles human wisdom. Peter, however, in his second letter, indicates that scoffers had already tackled the topic with the pseudo-omnipotence only the cynical possess: "Where is the promise of his coming? For ever since the fathers fell asleep, all things have continued as they were from the beginning of creation" (2 Pet. 3:4). Peter assures the scoffers that God needs no instruction on how to end things. He then gives some reasons for the delay. First, he points out that God is not subject to human conceptions of time: "But do not ignore this one fact, beloved, that with the Lord one day is as a thousand years, and a thousand years as one day" (2 Pet. 3:8). Before we think of this as some sort of cop-out, reflect on how completely enslaved we humans are to time periods. An Indian once said, "The white man's most wretched invention is the wristwatch." We are the ones with schedule problems, not God.

"But isn't two thousand years enough time for God?" someone will ask. Certainly it would be if we think only of the same set of people being constantly exposed to the fact of God. Perhaps, in God's view, the full value of Christ will arise only when human history has tried and exhausted every conceivable substitute for God. The true brilliance of Christ might appear only when he is seen in contrast to a long variety of systems and ideas. Eons might be required, in God's view, for every illusory dream of human progress to be shattered by the facts of man's sinful existence.

Jesus gave us some clues that his arrival might be delayed. In the delay of the bridegroom (Matt. 25:5) and the nobleman who journeys into a "far country" (Luke 19:12ff.) we hear Jesus say, "No one knows the hour!" The second appearance does not seem to lie at point X on any calendar; rather it seems to hover constantly over the history of the world.

God Keeps His Own Schedule

A second reason for the delay of Christ's return, according to Peter, is that the present heavens and earth are being *reserved* for fire (2 Pet. 3:7). The word "reserved" in the original means, literally, that destruction is "stored up," as a treasure would be kept in a vault for safe-keeping. This means that the destruction of the world is securely in God's hands. It is already decided upon as a present fact, but it is "being kept" for "a day of judgment and destruction of godless men."

In speaking of "being kept," Peter uses a present participle, indicating a continual keeping of the forces of destruction. The certainty of destruction is thus maintained on God's agenda as a continuously valid priority item to be used at his own discretion. Only God will decide when conditions are just right for Christ's return.

The Motive of Mercy

Another reason for a delay in the second appearance of Christ is that God mercifully allows us time to prepare for judgment:

> The Lord is not slow about his promise as some count slowness, but is forbearing toward you, not wishing that any should perish, but that all should reach repentance.
>
> 2 Peter 3:9

This is the attitude God has always had toward the wicked:

> As I live, says the Lord God, I have no pleasure in the death of the wicked, but that the wicked turn from his way and live; turn back, turn back from your evil ways.
>
> Ezekiel 33:11

God's redeeming love is at the heart of his holding back the destructive forces of the end time. He really wants people to prepare to enjoy his blessings. What more can God say to the wicked than he has already said in Christ? What more can God do for the unbeliever than he has done in sending Christ? Nothing, for in this action God has sent and testified to the best heaven can offer. So, God gives time.

Of course, if men encounter death before the final moment of the world, they must face God (Heb. 9:27). It is not morally healthy to presume on God's graciousness in granting time. We may reach the spiritual point of no return and find that even the maximum amount of time is of no value in softening a hardened heart. But it is comforting for the believer to know that God is so patient that he delays the most momentous event since Christ's first coming solely because he wants everyone to have an opportunity to repent.

He Is Able

The second coming, then, is the closing of the parentheses which opened at Bethlehem. The completion of God's great adventure of love lies on the horizon. He desires nothing more than to sustain believers until that day, so that all will enjoy the blessings of grace and complete salvation. He wants us to share in the security experienced by the apostle Paul, who could say, "I am not ashamed, for I know whom I have believed, and I am sure that he is able to guard until that Day what has been entrusted to me" (2 Tim. 1:12). It is Jesus who came, who is coming, and who is able to make his appearance a day of joy for the believer. His grace is therefore behind it all:

> The grace in which Christians stand is of a piece with the crown of glory they shall have at the end. It is not a question of the speedy occurrence of something wholly novel but the culmination of something already known.[2]

To this it might be added that the second appearance of Christ is not merely the occurrence of "something already known," but of *Someone* already known!

---

[1]See *An Eschatology of Victory* by J. Marcellus Kik, (Phillipsburg, N.J.: Presbyterian and Reformed Publishing Co., 1978), pp. 59-60.
[2]E.G. Selwyn, *The First Epistle of St. Peter* (London: Macmillan, 1969), pp. 111-112.

Experiencing the
10 *Resurrection*

The German writer Helmut Thielicke calls the resurrection of Christ the "magna carta" of his life. He affirms it is so important that it could well be posted before a believer's name on his driver's license:

"R"_____

(Fill in believer's name here)

The point is well-taken. We are "R" people in Christ. Can you imagine how personally powerful Christ's resurrection would be in your life if you really listened to what Jesus is trying to tell you about it?

This is the very point Jesus was trying to get across to John in his appearance to him on the island of Patmos (Rev. 1). "Fear not," he said, "I am the first and the last, and the living one: I died, and behold I am alive for evermore" (Rev. 1:17-18). "I am the living one," Jesus says. Jesus consistently tries to convince his followers that he is indeed the "resurrection and the life" (John 11:25). Because he lives, we shall always live. Yet he often finds us still uncertain. One of the primary purposes of the biblical teaching on the end times is to convince us of the power of the resurrection.

Two for the Road

Jesus' followers always seem to need this reassurance. Remember the two dispirited disciples traveling to the village of Emmaus (Luke 24:13ff.)? They were crushed in spirit because they had been hoping Jesus would redeem Israel. When he was crucified all their hopes apparently ended. They soon picked up a fellow traveler. This traveler was Jesus, but they failed to recognize him. Nothing in the text suggests that Jesus put any supernatural constraint on them to keep them from recognizing him. Their own "slowness of heart" (vs. 25) was probably responsible. Perhaps their grief, their sheer hopelessness, their lack of faith contributed. But Jesus persevered. He did for them what can be done for us. Back to the scriptures! He told them one more time what he had been telling his people all along (vs. 27). Finally they recognized the living Lord. Later the two recalled: "Did not our hearts burn within us while he talked to us on the road, while he opened to us the scriptures?" (Luke 24:32).

We still have such a Companion on the road. Jesus continues to try to convince us of his victory through the words of Scripture. He tells us he is alive, and because of that we shall live!

Joy on the Road

The doctrine of the resurrection is designed in Scripture to be far more than something discussed over Easter lilies once a year. The power of the resurrection comes to us on the road of life. This power transforms our dismal view which is constricted by too much "hereness and nowness" to a larger viewpoint. It is a day-in day-out affirmation that imparts joy in daily duties for Christ.

For example, when the apostle Peter urged elders of the church to be good shepherds of the flock, he began by mentioning that he was an "R-person"—the resurrection hope served as motivation for his daily tasks. He had a view of Christ's sufferings, but also, and most importantly, he knew that he at that present moment shared in the "glory to be revealed" (1 Pet. 5:1). The glorified Christ shares his glory to light up the path of daily duty.

When Peter wanted to ground believers in the apostles' doctrine instead of myths, he again referred to the resurrected glory of Christ (2 Pet. 1:12-18). This foretaste of glory is a present force directing us as we put on the Christian graces of 2 Peter 1:5-7. On the other hand, denying the resurrection has moral overtones of serious dimensions for the believer:

> What do I gain if, humanly speaking, I fought with beasts at Ephesus? If the dead are not raised, "Let us eat and drink, for tomorrow we die." Do not be deceived: "Bad company ruins good morals."
>
> 1 Corinthians 15:32-33

Without the perspective the resurrection gives to the Christian's life he might be tempted to live only for the day. He might give in to despair. By associating with such destructive ideas his whole moral life can be undermined.

The real problem in such a despairing outlook

though, is that it stems from inadequate ideas about God.

What Kind of God Is God?

Paul says in the section of Scripture just following that quoted above that wrong ideas about God are responsible for unbelief in the resurrection: "Come to your right mind, and sin no more. For some have no knowledge of God. I say this to your shame" (1 Cor. 15:34).

Sometimes interpreters who take this passage out of context think Paul is referring to evangelizing people with no knowledge of God. Paul certainly supports that idea, but here he is addressing believers who are ignorant of God's real purposes. Their moral problems are the result of failing to refer their lives to a God of resurrection power. They do not know the God of the resurrection, for in denying that the dead are raised they deny the power of God. This ineffectual God they believe in is not the God of Scripture.

Some minds apparently cannot take in so incredible a thought as the resurrection. So they limit God. When Paul was on trial before King Agrippa and Festus the Proconsul he felt called upon to exclaim: "Why is it thought incredible by any of you that God raises the dead?" (Acts 26:8). "What kind of God do you believe in anyway?" Paul seems to ask. Like Jesus, Paul has known the awesome power of the resurrection. He cannot help sharing what it will do for people.

What You Don't Know Can Hurt You

Ignorance is not bliss; it is danger. A group of Jewish aristocrats in the time of Christ belonged to a religious association called the Sadducees. This sect did not believe in the resurrection. What they did not know meant the difference between spiritual life and death. Yet these ancient skeptics tried to catch Jesus with a tricky puzzle about a woman who married a succession of seven brothers. The theological tricksters wanted to know whose wife she would be in the resurrection. Jesus' reply catches them in their own disbelief:

> "You are wrong, because you know neither the scriptures nor the power of God. For in the resurrection they neither marry nor are given in marriage, but are like angels in heaven. And as for the resurrection of the dead, have you not read what was said to you by God, 'I am the God of Abraham, and the God of Isaac, and the God of Jacob'? He is not God of the dead, but of the living."
>
> Matthew 22:29-32

God had been affirming life all along, but the Sadducees were not listening. What they did not know is that God's Word and God's power are behind the resurrection. God is not the God of the dead, but of the living.

Resurrection and Rapture

Mistaken ideas about God's willingness to raise the dead are often encountered in the writings of skeptics, but another confusing error is seen in the ideas of many religious writers. Great confusion exists about the number of resurrections, and their purpose. Modern dispensationalism holds that at least two resurrections will occur. The *New Scofield Reference Bible*[1] teaches there will be one resurrection for ordinary believers, and another for Old Testament saints and those killed for Christ during a period they call "The Great Tribulation." Anthony Hoekema, while rejecting this view, explains it as follows:

> The first phase of Christ's return will be the so-called *rapture* which will occur at any moment. At this time Christ does not come all the way to earth, but only part of the way . . . .Now the rapture of all God's people takes place: risen believers and transformed believers are caught up in the clouds to meet the descending Lord in the air.[2]

The idea of "The Great Tribulation" grows out of the prediction of Christ in Matthew 24:21 that the end will be preceded by intensely troubled times. Some premillennialists teach that this will precede the "rapture"; others say that it will follow the "rapture," and that the faithful will thus be spared the tribulation.

The main point is that the Bible supports only one general resurrection. Daniel 12:2-3 and John 5:28-29 are typical passages which show that we should not expect a series of resurrections.

But perhaps the more serious error in this thinking is that the so-called first resurrection at the "rapture" is really for this earth. In the most popular dispensational thinking, the resurrection at the rapture is only to take believers away during the tribulation. Then they are supposed to return to earth with Christ in order to be in on the millennial reign. Thus, the resurrection is not for heavenly existence, but for an earthly existence of a thousand years. Of course, after the thousand years, the dispensationalists say all believers will be part of the eternal heavenly order. They do not say where or how the obvious changes in adapting to such diverse environments will occur.

This teaching is a basic contradiction to the Bible position that resurrection is for a radically different environment—heaven. Our resurrection bodies are not designed for another stretch of earthly living. We know the earth is perishable (2 Pet. 3:10) and Paul says our resurrection life is designed for a nonperishable state (1 Cor. 15:47-50). It would be pointless to have a resurrection body, fitted by God for an imperishable situation, only to be consigned to a perishable earth. When Christ comes for his people they will be with him in a resurrection existence from that moment on (1 Thess. 4:17). Who would want to return to earth?

Eternal Life Begins Now

But how does the doctrine of the resurrection help us now? Is the resurrection life all future? No—its completion and the implementation of the spiritual body are in the future, but eternal life begins in this life.

In John 5, Jesus healed a man who had been afflicted for thirty-eight years. This miracle caused a hostile reaction among the religious authorities because Jesus "worked" on the Sabbath. Jesus proceeded to tell the offended authorities that God himself does such works, and even greater ones as well: "For just as the Father raises the dead and makes them alive, so the Son also makes alive those whom he wills to" * (John 5:21). Jesus then affirms that the resurrection life begins here and now: "Most assuredly I say to you that the one hearing my word and trusting him who sent me has eternal life and is not coming into judgment but has been transferred from death into life" *(John 5:24). The phrase "has eternal life" is a present tense in the original. It is apparently a divine quality of life which touches this life, here and now.

I do not understand everything about the nature of eternal life. Neither do I understand the vastness of the ocean; but I have touched it at the beach where it meets the land. Similarly, those who trust Jesus begin now to share in the quality of life characteristic of the Father and the Son.

Jesus also speaks of being "transferred" from death to life as a present experience (John 5:24). It is no less than resurrection from the death of sin and an embarking on the life God willingly shares with believers: "Most assuredly I say to you that an hour is coming and is now here when the dead shall hear the voice of God's Son and those who listen shall come alive" * (John 5:25). This must be what Paul meant when he told Timothy about Christ "who abolished death and brought life and immortality to light through the gospel" (2 Tim. 1:10).

Consider Yourselves Dead . . . and Alive

Paul spells out the practical importance of this for our present lives in Romans 6, where we discover that newness of life begins upon our baptism into Christ (6:3-9). Thus because God accepts our new life as a reality in Christ we are called upon to "Consider yourselves to be dead to sin and alive to God in Christ Jesus" (6:11). In other words, we should accept the fact that God is counting us alive, not because we have it all together and are sinless, but because God has accepted Christ's death as our death and Christ's life as our life. Lewis Smedes expresses this beautifully:

> What Paul wants us to understand is that when Christ arose, a new situation was created with a totally new character and a totally new future. He wants us to understand that we do not create the new situation by our decision, that its future does not rest with our diligence . . . . To speak of coming alive with Christ is to say that we are assigned to the new reality introduced by Christ's resurrection. Now we have to keep on choosing to be what we have already become.[3]

In other words, by resurrection power we have changed sides in the great battle against death and the Deceiver. We are not back at Headquarters yet; that is in the future. But we have changed sides and have new weapons. We have been put into a position where we can struggle. We have the assurance of victory. "We have to keep on choosing to be what we have already become."

Resurrection As a Future Event

We have seen how Christ's resurrection power is a present reality that helps us in our struggle against sin and death. But its major culmination will be future. It was just this sort of consideration that led certain skeptics to ask: "How are the dead raised? With what kind of body do they come?" (1 Cor. 15:35).

Some Greeks asked this question because they generally could not understand a bodily resurrection. Many Grecians were affected by the Platonic and Gnostic ideas that the body was inferior, a prison house for the soul. But Paul insisted that the body, which was created by God, would also be raised by him (1 Cor. 15:44). To be sure, the resurrected body would not be "the body of this flesh," but a spiritual body (vs. 44). Still, the concept bothered the Greeks. Even today there is widespread confusion over terms like spirit, soul, and body. A brief inquiry into these terms may prove helpful.

Soul, Spirit, Body

"Soul" (Greek *psuche*) in Greek thought meant the center of life, feeling, thought, or the vital force which resides in the body. In Plato the word takes on a special meaning, becoming pre-existent and immortal. It is interesting to note that the Bible never speaks of immortal souls. In fact it says only God has immortality (see 1 Tim. 6:14-16). However the coming of Jesus "brought life and immortality to light through the gospel" (2 Tim. 1:10). Plato considered the soul as far nobler than the body. Greek philosophers had a saying—*sōma sēma*—"te body is a tomb."

In the New Testament, "soul" often means "life" in the sense of vital life, not mere existence, (cf. Matt. 2:20; 10:39). Yet it is a life which cannot be destroyed by humans (Matt. 10:28). This passage, as well as Acts 2:27, teaches that the soul survives death (cf. also Rev. 6:9; 20:4).

"Spirit" (Greek *pneuma*) in Greek thought was quite vague, being thought of as the stuff of which souls were made, or simply an airy material with intelligence. The Hebrew *ruach* from the Old Testament really gives more substance to the term "spirit" in the New Testament. It often describes the Spirit of God, a powerful physical and moral presence (cf. Gen. 1:2; Isa. 61:1; Ps. 51:11).

In the New Testament, "spirit" reaches its widest application. It refers to what is essential to human life (Luke 8:55). It also refers to beings whose life does not require a body—evil beings (Luke 9:39), angels (Heb. 1:14), fallen beings (1 Pet. 3:19). God is called "spirit" in John 4:24.

Sometimes it is difficult to distinguish between soul and spirit. The writer of Hebrews says only the word of God can discern this distinction (Heb. 4:12). Existence as a bare soul or a bare spirit is not considered desirable for man in the New Testament. Paul prays, "May the God of peace himself sanctify you wholly; and may your spirit and soul and body be kept sound and blameless at the coming of our Lord Jesus Christ" (1 Thess. 5:23). The emphasis here is on the wholeness desired for Christians rather than separation into parts. It is considered essential that this wholeness be preserved.

Thus, bodily redemption is considered necessary in New Testament thought to complete all God has in mind for his people. It guarantees the integrity of personal survival. This body will not be the limited physical body we now have. It will be gloriously adapted to the new conditions awaiting us. As Paul says, "I tell you brethren: flesh and blood cannot inherit the kingdom of God, nor does the perishable inherit the imperishable" (1 Cor. 15:50). Our present physical bodies are inadequate for the new environment God has planned for us.

Paul lists four problems that must be overcome

before we can enter into our full inheritance as God's children (cf. 1 Cor. 15:38-50):[4]

(1) Our present bodies are perishable. We age, contract disease, have physical problems. Our appreciation of the life to come would be severely diminished if this condition were not corrected.

(2) We suffer a loss of dignity as we age and die physically.

(3) We become weak and are unable to respond to the many opportunities that exist for growing in service to God.

(4) Our bodies are natural. That is, they are adapted to life on this planet. Thus their limitations are obvious for knowing a greater environment.

Four Promises of the Resurrection

The resurrection is designed to overcome the four problems that hold us back from total enjoyment of God's new life. To further our joy, God will raise us with spirits and souls intact in bodies that are to be "changed" by God's power again (cf. 1 Cor. 15:38-50):[4]

(1) They will be incorruptible, immune to destruction. There will be no such concept as aging; we will be constantly refreshed physically.

(2) They will be glorious bodies, that is, possessing a splendor which comes only from God. Think of a God-designed body supremely capable of serving, giving, and loving God eternally.

(3) They will be bodies of power. Weakness and disability will be unknown. They will enable us to do whatever is needed to do God's will, with no limitations.

(4) They will be "spiritual bodies," entities adapted by God for the world of the spirit. They

will be perfectly attuned to their environment. No discordant temptations will interrupt the pleasure of living in the presence of God.

The Great Change

C. S. Lewis tells of the possible experience on the last Day of encountering some individual we have known on earth. The person is next to us, and we see him or her as they will be at the final climax of all things. Lewis suggests that the person will have undergone a change of such magnitude that we would either be as tempted to worship them as John was the angel, so shining, so glorious in their resurrection bodies; or, we would turn from then in unspeakable horror, so unprepared would we be for this drastic change.

> Lo! I tell you a mystery. We shall not all sleep, but we shall all be changed, in a moment, in the twinkling of an eye, at the last trumpet. For the trumpet will sound, and the dead will be raised imperishable, and we shall be changed.
>
> 1 Corinthians 15:51-52

Still there remains this daily need: "Therefore, my beloved brethren, be steadfast, immovable, always abounding in the work of the Lord, knowing that in the Lord your labor is not in vain" (1 Cor. 15:58).

Of such daily duties great changes come!

---

[1]C. I. Scofield, ed., *New Scofield Reference Bible, King James Version* (New York: Oxford University Press, 1967), p. 1250.

[2]Anthony A. Hoekema, *The Bible and the Future* (Grand Rapids, Mich.: Eerdmans Publishing Co., 1979), pp. 164-165.

[3]Lewis B. Smedes, *All Things Made New* (Grand Rapids, Mich.: Eerdmans Publishing Co., 1970), pp. 138-139.

[4]Compare the discussion in Bernard Ramm's *Them He Glorified* (Grand Rapids, Mich.: Eerdmans Publishing Co., 1963).

11 Facing the Judgment

Queen Victoria of Great Britain celebrated her Diamond Jubilee on June 22, 1897. Cavalry from every part of the globe marched in a great parade in London. Eleven colonial governors, Hussars, Lancers, Sikhs, Chinese, Malays, Nigerians, and West Indians marched before the Queen. While millions cheered, Victoria rode in a carriage drawn by eight beautiful, cream-colored horses. A reporter from the London *Times* was present. As the cheering went on and on, he sensed an "aura of self-congratulation in the air." The reporter sat down and wrote a poem, which was printed in the *Times* the next day:

> God of our fathers, known of old—
> Lord of our far-flung battle-line—
> Beneath whose awful hand we hold
> Dominion over palm and pine—
> Lord God of Hosts, be with us yet,
> Lest we forget, lest we forget!
>
> Far-called our navies melt away—
> On dune and headland sinks the fire

Lo, all our pomp of yesterday
Is one with Nineveh and Tyre!
Judge of the Nations, spare us yet.
Lest we forget, lest we forget![1]

This poem, Rudyard Kipling's *The Recessional,* was the first dark note heralding the death of an empire that seemed indestructible.

The note of judgment rings through history as nations rise and fall, but it also has a final sound. The thought has enormous power to concentrate life upon reality. The biblical idea of judgment calls mankind to evaluate the difference between what is pomp and what is permanent.

Joy at Judgment?

How can something that sounds as threatening as judgment be a source of joy? Can the concept of joy be connected with what evokes images of tension, suspense, definitive evaluation, and possible rejection? Strangely enough, judgment is often a prayer that goes up from God's people: "O Sovereign Lord, holy and true, how long before thou wilt judge and avenge our blood on those who dwell upon the earth?" (Rev. 6:10).

Actually, every prayer for Christ to return is also a prayer for judgment. The coming of Christ and judgment are two aspects of the same event. Neither exists without the other. Since the coming of Christ is considered to be a joyous event for believers, then the connected idea of judgment can be expected to impart joy.

The apostle to the Gentiles used the thought this way when he wrote to the young church at Thessalonica. They were being persecuted severely, and Paul says the coming of Christ will mean "rest"

116

for them (2 Thess. 1:7). Paul then describes how Christ's coming will mean a judgment of condemnation for those who do not know God (vs. 8).

Judgment was not used by New Testament writers to frighten Christians. For them it meant deliverance and joy, for it would vindicate their suffering for the faith and bring divine affirmation of their way of life. It meant the triumph of right over wrong, good over evil. But how can Christians, who are after all quite imperfect people, look forward to such a day? It is because God is able to be both just and justifier in Christ.

Just and Justifier

How can God be just—that is thoroughly righteous and holy—if he intends to forgive believers who are really guilty? We would not permit an earthly judge to let the guilty go. We would insist that the full force of the law be applied. Should we not insist that God be perfectly fair and just? Is that not what true justice is all about?

The central problem for God, according to the analysis in Romans, is how God can be both just and justifier of the guilty. This is a problem which has no human solution, and might thereby be a frightening situation indeed. Fortunately, however, there is a divine solution:

> Since all have sinned and fall short of the glory of God, they are justified by his grace as a gift, through the redemption which is in Christ Jesus, whom God put forward as an expiation by his blood, to be received by faith. This was to show God's righteousness, because in his divine forbearance he had passed over former sins; it was to prove at

the present time that he himself is righteous
and that he justifies him who has faith in
Jesus.

Romans 3:23-26

The last thought in this section (vs. 26) is obscure for the English reader who does not realize
that the words "righteous" and "justified" are from
a common root in Greek. Taking that into account
it is possible to translate the thought this way: "It
was to prove at the present time that he is just and
justifier of the one who has faith in Jesus." Because of Jesus, God can be "just" and still "justify" sinners. To justify here means to pronounce
them "not guilty." They can be treated this way
only because Jesus has accepted the penalty of our
guilt upon himself. Thus God himself solves the
problem of judgment for us. This great fact is insisted upon by apostolic writers in passage after
passage. The faithfulness of God will see us
through even the day of Judgment.

God's fidelity is our greatest hope for coming
through that Day. That is why, above all, we must
hold on to our Father. Consider how strongly this
is affirmed in the following passages. To the Corinthians, as they await "the revealing of our Lord
Jesus Christ," Paul wrote that God "will sustain
you to the end, guiltless in the day of our Lord
Jesus Christ. God is faithful, by whom you were
called into the fellowship of his Son, Jesus Christ
our Lord" (1 Cor. 1:7-9). To the Philippians: "I am
sure that he who began a good work in you will
bring it to completion at the day of Jesus Christ"
(Phil. 1:6). And to the Thessalonians: "May the
God of peace himself sanctify you wholly; and
may your spirit and soul and body be kept sound

and blameless at the coming of our Lord Jesus Christ. He who calls you is faithful, and he will do it" (1 Thess. 5:23-24).

"He who calls you is faithful, and he will do it." What a gratifying idea! The faithfulness of God is what establishes our confidence in our encounter with judgment, not our own merit or excellence.

Confidence at Judgment

You may have heard sermons which depicted everyone, believers and unbelievers alike, standing before God on Judgment Day in great suspense. Believers are said to be in as much uncertainty as unbelievers. Would you find this position supported by New Testament authors? Not at all! Notice Paul:

> Henceforth there is laid up for me the crown of righteousness, which the Lord, the righteous judge, will award to me on that Day, and not only to me but also to all who have loved his appearing.
>
> 2 Timothy 4:8

John puts it even more confidently:

> So we know and believe the love God has for us . . . . In this is love perfected with us, that we may have confidence for the day of judgment, because as he is so are we in this world. There is no fear in love, but perfect love casts out fear. For fear has to do with punishment, and he who fears is not perfected in love. We love because he first loved us.
>
> 1 John 4:16-19

119

The ingredient which motivates us to have confidence is knowing we are loved by God. That is why we know that we share a relationship with God just like Jesus did ("because as he is so are we in this world"). God loves us as sons and daughters just as the Father loves the Son. Let us never let this love go, for it gives us confidence for the greatest encounter we will ever face.

Not Coming Into Judgment

In his discussion of the life-giving power of the Son in John 5, Jesus makes a significant statement: "Truly, truly I say to you, he who hears my word and believes him who sent me, has eternal life; he does not come into judgment, but has passed from death to life" (John 5:24). If the Christian has eternal life, and does not come into judgment, how do we account for passages like 1 Corinthians 4:5, 2 Corinthians 5:10 and others which obviously teach that believers will have to appear before the judgment seat of Christ?

In answering this question we must avoid committing the error of the dispensationalists who argue for as many as four judgments. This has no support in Scripture at all, and ends up creating more confusion than anything else. We must look elsewhere for the answer to this involved question.

Jesus has stated absolutely that the believer will not come into judgment (John 5:24). Paul says in Romans 8:1, "There is therefore now no condemnation for those who are in Christ Jesus." Yet we have passages obviously teaching we shall have to appear before Christ. The answer must be that we do not enter into judgment *as unbelievers do,* to be condemned. Since we are in Christ, we do not enter judgment in the sense of condemnation because

120

Christ has already accepted our condemnation upon himself. (Rom. 5:8-9). We must appear before Christ for a different reason than condemnation. In fact, the Bible suggests that believers will appear in judgment to have their stewardship evaluated, not to be censured.

Incentive for Stewardship

There is no comfort in this concept for unfaithful, irresponsible Christians. Judgment, for believers, is a powerful incentive for responsible discipleship. In fact, Paul says that judgment by the Lord is actually designed to keep us from being condemned along with the world (1 Cor. 11:32). Whether he is referring to a judgment in this life or the life to follow, the principle is the same. The Lord encourages responsibility. When we love Jesus we want to appear before him as responsible, loving disciples. Such a sense of responsibility was partly why Paul engaged in evangelism (2 Cor. 5:10-11), although his primary motivation is based on Christ's great love (2 Cor. 5:14). This inner motivation controlled his life; his desire to be responsible serves as an outer check.

On being a builder. Another aspect of our stewardship has to do with having the attitude of builders—that is, being constructive. In 1 Corinthians 3:10-17 Paul's analysis of those who serve bases judgment upon whether one builds or destroys. The builder, even the often ineffective one, is saved (vs. 15); but the destroyer is lost with no hope (vss. 16-17). Presumably this is because the destroyer of fellowship is really doing the devil's work and not the Lord's. No matter how we look at it, we are either builders or destroyers. We are either trying to build up, encourage, and maintain

121

the Spirit's unity (Eph. 4:1ff.), or we are tearing down, ripping apart, and splitting. Which type are we?

An illuminating way to discover our attitude is to ask what we look for in people. Do we generally look for the bad, the evil, the weakness in others and dwell on these? Or do we look for what may be built upon? Christ would have his people look for what may be built upon for good in the lives of others. Notice Paul's words to the Ephesians:

> Since I have heard of your faith in the Lord Jesus and your love directed toward all the saints, I have not ceased expressing thanks for you when I mention you on the occasion of my prayers. *

Eph. 1:15-16

What is Paul doing? Identifying what could be built upon! He could build on faith and love, so he looked for it and commended it. Were they perfect? Sinless? Not at all, but they were blessed with a gentle teacher who discovered what could be built upon in their lives. So Christ challenges us to be builders in others' lives. We must remember that even the most fumbly-fingered builder is saved, but the most efficient destroyer is lost. Christ is more sensitive to the attitude of his followers than to their efficiency.

When did we see thee? Another area of responsibility to be evaluated when we appear before Christ is that of serving others. The entire judgment scene of Matthew 25:31-46 focuses on this idea. While this passage teaches universal truth applicable to all people (note 25:32), it also reinforces the Christian's confidence that serving his fellow man is serving Christ. Some persons in Matthew 25 seem to feel no obligation toward those in need because they are oblivious to their suffering. Others were sensitive enough to be relievers of the pain and anguish around them. At judgment they discovered that they had come to the aid of Christ himself!

Christ is saying here that one is not a Christian because he lives and moves in a Christian environment, or because his friends, parents, and teachers are Christians. One is a Christian when he dedicates his heart and life to living for God and serves others in his name. These people see Christ on every hand. For them, the mention of judgment does not cast doubt on their expectations but encourages them to look forward to offering up responsible stewardship to the Lord.

The Day of Reality

The day of Judgment does not add a new reality; it merely confirms what already exists. People do not become unbelievers on that day; they are already unbelievers. At judgment God merely reveals the terrible reality of their situation. We cannot set up our own autonomous reign in the middle of God's kingdom. We cannot be squatters on God's property and not have our hand called at some point. It is possible to lose. As C. S. Lewis said, "There are finally two kinds of people; those who say to God: 'Thy will be done.' And those to whom God must say: 'Thy will be done.' "[2]

Paul warns the young believers in Thessalonica not to be taken in by the complacency and laxity of the unbelieving world around them: "When people say, 'There is peace and security,' then sudden destruction will come upon them" (1 Thess. 5:3). The idea of judgment is that a final, irrevocable line is drawn between this world and the next. Judgment speaks not of complacency but of decision. Judgment calls on us to break with the world's concepts of peace and security.

Elie Wiesel's little book *Night* has a chilling truth in it along this line. Wiesel tells of Jews living in the little village of Sighet, Hungary during World War II. A group of foreign Jews were deported from the town, supposedly to go to work in forced labor camps in Germany. One of them, Moche, escaped from the Germans and came back to tell of his experiences. The Gestapo had forced them to dig their own graves, but Moche was only wounded and managed to get away. Finding his way back to the village he spent his days trying to warn the remaining Jews to flee. They laughed at him: "Poor fellow, he's gone quite mad."

Then German troops entered the town. At first the Jews were frightened, but as nothing happened right away, they became complacent again. They said, "Well, there you are . . . There are your Germans! What do you think of them? Where is their famous cruelty?" Wiesel adds: "The Germans were already in the town, the Fascists were already in power, the verdict had already been pronounced, yet the Jews of Sighet continued to smile."[3]

The party will soon be over—forever! But God stands ready to justify, to give confidence and joy, even on that Great Day.

[1]Rudyard Kipling, *The Recessional*, lines 1–12.
[2]C.S. Lewis, *The Best of C.S. Lewis, The Great Divorce* (Grand Rapids, Mich.: Baker Book House, 1969), p. 156.
[3]Elie Wiesel, *Night* (New York: Avon Bard Books, 1972).

12 Avoiding Eternal Punishment

The Italian poet Dante Alighieri, in his imaginative *Inferno,* describes the gates of hell as inscribed with these words:

I am the Way into the City of Woe
I am the Way to a Forsaken People
I am the Way into Eternal Sorrow . . .
Abandon All Hope Ye Who Enter Here.[1]

But no effort of medieval imagination can touch the real horror of hell—it is where God will never appear. It is the place where cunning rebels against God can sorrow at their own success in evading him.

Warnings Are Serious

The biblical doctrines of the last things mention much of gain and glory, both here and hereafter. But there is another side, a dark side. This is the doctrine of eternal sorrow, eternal loss. It cannot be deleted without serious distortion of the future possibilities for mankind. No pleasure comes from this consideration, but it is essential. What foolish-

125

ness it would be to ignore the plain warnings of Scripture about this future danger. Warnings are meant to be listened to seriously.

A few years ago when our family lived in Louisiana, a hurricane began brewing off the Gulf shore. Weather forecasters dubbed it "Camille" and sternly warned all local residents to abandon the area. Some people in Biloxi decided to ignore the warnings. They threw a big "hurricane party" to make merry through the storm. After midnight, at the height of the festivities, a tidal wave thirty feet high roared ashore like a freight train headed for the apartment house where the party was going on. The building was smashed off its foundation in seconds. No trace was found of the party-goers. Warnings are meant to be taken seriously.

The biblical warnings on hell are to be taken with equal seriousness. All sorts of barbaric motives are attributed to believers who take this doctrine at face value. No doubt some have had a morbid spirit of rejoicing at the destruction of unrepentant sinners, but this is not God's attitude, nor the attitude of true believers. "As I live, says the Lord God, I have no pleasure in the death of the wicked, but that the wicked turn from his way and live" (Ezek. 33:11). God derives pleasure from seeing the wicked turn away from death to life. The same is true of those who present the biblical ideas on final punishment, if their spirit is that of God. It is a serious warning, but it is offered in hope that the person without God will turn and find life in him.

Did Jesus Believe in Hell?

Jesus taught that it is possible to ignore God's

offer of grace and be eternally lost. In fact, no one person in the Bible spoke more definitively on the subject of hell than Jesus. Other than one reference in James 3:6, Jesus was the only one in the Bible to use the term *gehenna* to refer to hell. This is a particularly strong term based upon the Hebrew for "Valley of the Sons of Hinnom." This valley, which was adjacent to Jerusalem, had been the site of horrible immolations to idols. In later days it had become a garbage dump with smoldering fires burning constantly. *Gehenna* connoted a grimy, polluted destination for refuse. Thus hell, in Jesus' usage, carries the imagery of an eternal garbage heap, a wasteland of souls. Some of his references to this possible destiny are found in Matthew 5:22, 29, 30; Mark 9:43, 45, 47; Luke 12:5 and other places in the synoptic Gospels.

Jesus used other terms to describe hell. He spoke of its separation from Jesus, the "light of the world," by describing it as "outer darkness" (Matt. 8:12). He stressed the indescribably painful difference between heaven and hell by speaking of it as an "unquenchable fire" (Mark 9:43) and "eternal fire" (Matt. 18:8, 25:41). He warned that the evil would "perish" or "be destroyed" (Matt. 7:13; John 3:16). Obviously, Jesus took the idea of hell very seriously.

Jesus did not refer to hell as a stock argument to support weak premises. He used the concept of hell to impress men with the serious consequences of ignoring his summons to obey God. He referred to hell to implore men to grasp the true dangers of reckless sinning. In Matthew 5:29 he warned that "It is better that you lose one of your members than that your whole body be thrown into hell."

Jesus is not counseling self-mutilation. He is saying that sin must be dealt with in drastic ways. No half-hearted efforts will get to the center of the matter. Jesus stressed the danger of hanging onto sin and thereby risking total rejection before God.

How to Avoid Hell

Be sensitive to the needs of others. According to Jesus, hell will be populated with those who maintain a cold indifference to other's welfare. He used the shocking story of the rich man (Luke 16:19ff.) to show the complete reversal that hell would effect in the lives of the self-satisfied who were insensitive to others' needs. The rich man is tormented in the after-life because he neglected the needy in this life. The judgment scene in Matthew 25:31ff. centers on the same theme. Eternal fire, prepared for the devil and his angels (not mankind), is the destiny of those who ignore the distressed of this world (vs. 41). In bypassing the needy, insignificant as they are in worldly eyes, we make void our right to enter heaven. Jesus' emphasis is that we must learn to look for him in the needs of our fellow humans.

Forego the easy route. Another major emphasis in Jesus' teaching on hell is the necessity of preparing for the new life in the Spirit. Most people, he warned, are looking for an easy route to glory. But they are sadly deluded:

Enter by the narrow gate; for the gate is wide and the way is easy, that leads to destruction, and those who enter it are many. For the gate is narrow and the way is hard, that leads to life, and those who find it are few.

Matthew 7:13-14

Jesus does not mean that the road of life is obscure—actually it is much too clear for most of us! He is informing those inclined to spiritual dabbling that heaven will be discovered only by those who are serious about it.

The word "destruction" in this passage is from the Greek word *apōleia*. By "destruction" or "perishing" the New Testament writers do not mean annihilation. The shade of meaning is toward "lostness" and "waste." In fact, the verb form is translated "wasted" in Mark 14:4. With this thought in mind, Paul's point on the destiny of the disobedient becomes clear: "They shall suffer the punishment of eternal destruction and exclusion from the presence of the Lord and from the glory of his might, when he comes on that day" (2 Thess 1:9-10). The spiritually unprepared waste not only their present but their entire future also. Hell is seen once more to be a blighted wasteland.

Don't give up. Hell represents the ultimate negative, the loss of all that is worth having. While we may be tempted by discouragement to abandon faith, the loss represented by unbelief should help us keep Christ at the center of our lives. The writer of Hebrews warns against spiritual fatigue by speaking of hell as the loss of that which is of immense value. Unbelief will result in not entering into God's rest (Heb. 3:18-19). Faith means obtaining permanent possession of all that our souls are meant to be; but unbelief means total loss:

> Do not throw away your confidence, which has a great reward. For you have need of endurance, so that you may do the will of God and receive what is promised . . . . But

we are not of those who shrink back and are
destroyed, but of those who have faith and
keep their souls.

Hebrews 10:35-36, 39

Hell is ruin, loss, destruction, waste, and perpetual death.

Appreciate life. The book of Revelation uses the
most graphic language about hell. One of its images is of hell as "the lake of fire" (Rev. 20:14),
which is then explained to mean "the second
death." The first death is physical, separation from
our earthly bodies. The second death is spiritual
separation from God. The only way that this second death can be defeated is through Christ. If we
appreciate life in Christ fully enough to resist evil,
the second death has no power over us (Rev. 2:11).
Hell means the absolute abyss of future experiences. But God's free gift of life (Rom. 6:23) defeats the second death.

Two Objections Considered

Hell presents such a spectacle of blasted hopes
that it is no wonder that many recoil at the
thought. As we have seen, the biblical information
itself is not presented with any rejoicing, but as the
sober reality that it is possible to lose everything.
The dangers of spiritual unpreparedness, deliberate
sinfulness, and sheer indifference can lead to ruin
and a hopeless future. It is no good offering lame
rationalizations, such as "we have our hell here on
earth." To be separated from God makes that statement true enough, for hell's outreach touches lives
even here and now. But to deny that hell is also a
possible future is a perilous attempt to dispose of
what God has seen fit to establish as a reality.

Hell and a god of love. One objection to the concept of hell is that it is difficult to put the gracious God and hell together in one sentence. How could a loving God create such a place as hell? Would this not represent a defeat for his love? Could not a truly loving God have done more to keep men from such a fate?"

Crucial to this question is what is meant by "loving"? If "loving" means indulgence and condoning every sort of transgression with no expectation of repentance, then we can safely say that God does not offer that kind of love. Paul addresses this question at least twice in the book of Romans. In chapter 11 he tries to get across the double concept of God's kindness and severity: "Note then the kindness and severity of God" (11:22). For those who depart from God there is severity; for those who approach him there is kindness. Paul is saying that we cannot suppose God to be indifferent to our reception of his grace. Paul also refers to God's severity in Romans 1:18, where he uses the phrase "the wrath of God." This does not mean that God's attitude is one of petulance or petty grudge-keeping. On the contrary, his wrath is his fixed hostility to sin. Forgive sin, yes! Condone sin, never!

Imagine a painter so dedicated he could not tolerate falseness in art. Imagine a doctor so committed he would not hide or dismiss a single defect in the health of a patient. Imagine a machine so finely tuned that it screened out every defect in a factory inspection line. if we can conceive of these, then we can also conceive of a Being so grounded in reality that he can dismiss no evil, nor overlook it.

Consider also that this Being whom we call God

131

has provided a soul-saving solution whereby no one needs to hold onto his sinfulness. He gave his own Son as an act of love, so that no person need perish eternally (John 3:16). If one persists in hanging onto his sinfulness, he rejects the love of God. He sins against what love has provided. Hell is our own choice when we refuse the cleansing love of God. The very nature of freely-given love allows the one loved to refuse that love. Who doesn't hold in distaste that individual who insists on forcing his love or attention on some unwilling object? Such smother-love is seldom appreciated or returned. Genuine love always carries with it the right to refuse to be loved. God's love is not cheap. It cost him his Son. But it is a love which can be rejected. To refuse it is to accept hell, but refuse it we can. God cannot love enough to save the unwilling. You cannot keep life in what is determined to die. "There is a sin unto death" (1 John 5:16 KJV).

'How Could I Be Happy?

A perplexed questioner asked me, "How could I be happy in heaven if someone I loved on the earth was sent to hell?" First, we cannot limit God's power to make us happy. While this capacity may be beyond comprehension, it is no less real. As Paul affirms: "What no eye has seen, nor ear heard, nor the heart of man conceived, what God has prepared for those who love him" (1 Cor. 2:9).

Second consider that our viewpoint may be significantly altered by our new status in the presence of God himself, for in heaven all things will be new (Rev. 21:5). If you have children, do you remember how you felt about your first child before he or she was born? At best it would have all

132

been vague and imaginary. But once that child was in the family you could not then imagine life without him. Now suppose that in the future as a child of the resurrection (Luke 20:36) you have just such an actual experience that transforms your imagination to one of reality. You are in a state where what you perceived to be a key relationship on earth may not appear in heaven to have the same value. Jesus seems to be saying in Luke 20:34ff. that something important changes from this life to the next, that being a son of *God* is the relationship that defines happiness in the life to come. We may very well discover that in terms of this "key" we did not really know the one we loved upon the earth. It would be inevitable, then, since we do not share this "key relationship," that we drift apart from such persons.

I myself have had such an experience in this life. I was very close to a certain person when I was young. I thought we had an excellent relationship; there was little we could not share. We were separated in young adulthood and it was years later when we met. We were no longer close. The silence was frustrating, but little existed to unite us at that point. We have traveled diverging paths, and each passing year only pushed us farther apart. I never thought I would be a virtual stranger in the presence of that former friend, but it was so. Will we not find, in a similar way, that those who have chosen paths that diverge from the life of God are strangers after all, strangers in that one vital area which must be shared for life to go on in the presence of God? Would we not sense the inappropriateness of such a relationship, a relationship which we have absolutely outgrown?

In Retrospect

This chapter has purposedly avoided being a topography of hell. Leave that to Dante and others of imagination! The real facts of the Bible are quite frightening enough. It is also frightening to see that human beings can be so indifferent, unprepared, and reckless in sinning that eternity itself must confirm their preferences. If hell is not enough to frighten such persons, perhaps our sharing with them the lavish love of God might attract them to him. This is a love that brings the dead in sin to life again (Eph. 2:1ff.), and then confirms that love for eternity.

As for those who persist in choosing hell, it is not much of a choice; it is the very negation of choice. But choose we must, for we cannot hold on to hell and have heaven. In my opinion, no better observation on that choice exists, outside the biblical data, than these words of the late English scholar C. S. Lewis:

> Evil can be undone, but it cannot "develop" into good. Time does not heal it . . . . It is still "either-or!" If we insist on keeping Hell we shall not see Heaven: if we accept Heaven we shall not be able to retain even the smallest and most intimate souvenirs of Hell.[2]

---

[1]Dante Alighieri, *Inferno*, canto 3, lines 1–9.

[2]C.S. Lewis, *The Great Divorce* (New York: Macmillan, 1945), preface.

13 *Inheriting Heaven*

The English Rennaisance scholar Sir Thomas More wrote a book about an ideal human community. When deciding upon a title he came up with the unique idea of coining a new word—*Utopia*. Sir Thomas got the word by combining two Greek words, *eutopia* (a good place) and *outopia* (no place). More was a better prophet than he thought, for humans have not been able to construct the perfect society. There is "no place" on earth where human community is perfectible. Walter Lippman reflects the disillusionment of those who have tried to set the world aright in a human manner:

> We ourselves were so sure that at long last a generation had arisen, keen and eager, to put this disorderly earth to right . . . . We meant so well. We tried so hard, and look what we have made of it . . . . What is required is a new kind of man.[1]

A Colony of Heaven

Although mankind must look to someone other than itself to form the ideal community, a colony of

135

a spiritual Utopia does exist today. It is not some esoteric commune, but ordinary people who are taking God's call seriously. The apostle Paul said that Christians are presently citizens of heaven (Phil. 3:20). The members of the body of Christ are a colony of heaven planted on this earth for the present. While this colony is not yet what it will be, it can still point the way to that final reality, the real *eutopia*.

The present reality of this colony is also evident from the fact that *angels,* generally considered heavenly beings, also populate the present. These mysterious beings are God's messengers (cf. Rev. 1:1). They attend God in his heavenly splendor (Rev. 8:1-2). But from the beginning of Scripture to the end, angels also tinge the earthly existence of the faithful with a heavenly glow. They carried the message to Abraham that God had chosen him to be the father of the faithful. An angel announced the birth of Jesus and his resurrection as well. It is worth noting that while we will apparently share heaven with these glorious beings, we will not ourselves be changed into angels. In heaven, Jesus says, we will be *like* the angels (Matt. 22:30).

The Inheritance

Members of the colony of heaven are actually heirs who will receive all the blessings of the final order. Jesus Christ tells us that he is the rightful heir (Mark 12:1-11), and his apostle says that all believers are joint-heirs with him:

> For you did not receive the spirit of slavery to fall back into fear, but you have received the spirit of sonship. When we cry, "Abba! Father!" it is the Spirit himself bearing wit-

ness with our spirit that we are children of God, and if children, then heirs, heirs of God and fellow heirs with Christ, provided we suffer with him in order that we may also be glorified with him.

Romans 8:15-17

This inheritance is available to all who will accept God's call in Christ. It is not like inheriting some useless item from an eccentric uncle. It is inheriting all that is glorious. It is a new quality of life—one that begins in the here and now, according to the apostle John: "This is the testimony, that God gave us eternal life, and this life is in his Son. He who has the Son has life; he who has not the Son of God has not life" (1 John 5:11-12). But the final form of eternal life will not appear until heaven is actually inherited. "We are God's children now; it does not yet appear what we shall be, but . . . we shall be like him, for we shall see him as he is" (1 John 3:2).

The Bible's emphasis on the Christian's inheritance is that it is with Him, and not on heaven as a place. Although we will note that issue later, Scripture emphasizes that our inheritance is "in Christ." The hope is centered on being with a Person, not inheriting a place. Notice the desire of the author of Psalm 73:25-26:

> Whom have I in heaven but thee?
>   And there is nothing upon earth
>   that I desire besides thee.
> My flesh and my heart may fail,
>   but God is the strength of my heart
>   and my portion for ever.

"Portion" here is the Hebrew word usually translated "inheritance." The psalmist does not think of heaven so much as the One in heaven.

The New Testament repeats this stress. The famous passage in John 14, so often quoted with a focus upon the *place* prepared, actually places Christ in the forefront. Having Christ is the real promise; the place only makes possible that togetherness with Christ:

> In my Father's house are many rooms [Greek "dwelling places"]; if it were not so, would I have told you that I go to prepare a place for you? And when I go and prepare a place for you, I will come again and will take you to myself, that where I am you may be also.
>
> John 14:2-3

Our heritage is where Jesus is. We may trust that the place will more than fulfill our expectations, not because of its ornateness but because of Who is there. When heaven, therefore, is described as having streets of gold, we know that this is only a way of heightening the value of dwelling with Jesus. After all, one may tire of gold, as did King Midas; but no one will tire of being with God. As Paul says the real joy of everything shifting into its final phase is that it means "we shall always be with the Lord" (1 Thess. 4:17).

A Reservation for Us

It has always been hard for me to stop for food or lodging on a trip. I always want to make a few more miles before stopping. One spring my wife Joyce and I were on our way to the nation's capital to see the famous Cherry Blossom Festival. A few miles south of Washington Joyce spotted a "Vacancy" sign and suggested things would be pretty crowded up ahead. "Shouldn't we stop while there's an opening?" she asked.

"No, honey," I said, "there's bound to be a motel even closer, and we can make twenty more miles before we have to stop." Well, we drove all the way to Washington, all the way through Washington, and all the way to Baltimore, seeing nothing but "*No Vacancy*" signs. Finally, in Baltimore, we found a dubious rooming house with a vacancy. It was one of those places with hot and cold running cockroaches. But it didn't matter; I wasn't destined to sleep that night, anyway. Who can sleep when his wife is saying "I told you so" all night? I was cured. From that night on I called ahead and made reservations. I must admit that my wife was right—it's a much more pleasant trip knowing there is a nice place waiting for you at the end of the day's travel.

Peter actually mentions something along this same line in reference to heaven:

> Blessed be the God and father of our Lord Jesus Christ! By his great mercy we have been born anew to a living hope through the resurrection of Jesus Christ from the dead, and to an inheritance which is imperishable, undefiled, and unfading, *kept* in heaven for you (author's emphasis).
>
> 1 Peter 1:3-4

The word translated *kept* is a perfect participle in the original. The meaning of the perfect in Greek is that something has happened in the past but it is still effective in the present. Our inheritance is available, or as we would say "reserved." How encouraging to know that at the final stop, when your travels through this life end, your reservation is made and waiting for you.

The next verse is also instructive. First Peter 1:5 says that this reservation is for those whose faith enables God's power to guard them in this life so that we may show up to claim our reservation. It will be worthwhile to claim it! For Peter tells us that our inheritance is "imperishable, undefiled, and unfading." These three descriptive terms are truly beautiful in the original. They all begin with the Greek letter alpha and have a lovely sound when pronounced. It is quite a memorable combination and you can easily imagine early Christians saying, "my inheritance is *aphthartos, amiantos,* and *amarantos.*"[2]

Aphthartos: the imperishable inheritance. This first term refers back to the land inheritance which God gave Israel in Canaan. Though granted to them by God, it was often ravaged by invading armies because of Israel's sinfulness. *Aphthartos* means "unravaged" by invading armies. No hostile forces will take our inheritance from us. No argumentative wrangling will disgrace our heritage. The word also carries the connotation of being indestructible. In a day of transient fads it is difficult to find anything permanent. But in our heavenly inheritance we will finally know real permanence and unending security.

Amiantos: the undefiled inheritance. Isn't it detestable when vandals mar a work of art? How do you feel when you find your freshly mowed lawn strewn with beer cans and whiskey bottles? Are you disgusted to see beautiful lakes choked with polution? And, what about the moral pollution all around us? Truth is perverted, "love" is used to manipulate rather than bless. But there will be no such defacing of our heavenly inheritance, for no defiling person will be there to mar the landscape. Spiritual vandals have their opportunity in this life to come to the Lord. The life to come is for those who appreciate *the* beauty of being with him.

Amarantos: the unfading inheritance. Once the rose was a beautiful, fragrant living flower. Now, pressed between the pages of an old Bible, it had become yellowed and faded. When it was fresh, so was the person who wore it on that day so long ago. But now they are both old. Rupert Brook has caught the theme with great poignancy:

> Whatever passes not, in the great hour,
> nor all my passion, all my prayers,
> have power to hold them with me through
> the gate of Death . . . .
> the best I've known,
> Stays here, and changes, breaks, grows old,
> is blown about the winds of the world,
> and fades from brains of living men,
> and dies. Nothing remains.[3]

Ah, but Peter says that there is something that remains—something fresh, unfading, ever new. It is our inheritance, which is our ongoing relationship with God and Christ. This relationship stays fresh and exciting always. We can never experience boredom or ennui with God. In this life, relationships with friends and sometimes even with family members can grow stale. Human love can fade. But our relationships in heaven will remain as fresh as spring.

The Place of the Inheritance

While we have noted that the biblical emphasis is upon a Person to be with, not the place, Scripture still speaks of heaven as a "place." Surely there is something figurative about this kind of language, for locales and spaces seem out of place in a realm where time and space are no more. But perhaps human language offers no alternatives. Again it is Peter who says, "According to his promise we wait for new heavens and a new earth in which righteousness dwells" (2 Pet. 3:13).

Sometimes it is argued that Peter and other New Testament writers refer only to a refurbished earth and sky. Heaven, it is said, will not be really *new,* but the old earth and sky cleansed and renewed. One such argument is based on the Greek word *kainos,* used in these passages. This word is supposed to mean "renewed," not "new," in this context. The Greek word for "new in kind," we are told, is *neos,* which is not used to describe the "new heavens and a new earth." These distinctions between *kainos* and *neos* may have held up in classical times, but they seem to have had no validity at the time the New Testament was written.

The two words are actually used synonymously in the New Testament. For example, both *neos* and *kainos* are used to describe the new covenant in Hebrews and 8:8 and 12:24. Surely if there had been this difference between the two words, both could not be applied to the covenant of Christ. John 19:41 tells us that the tomb in which Jesus was laid was a new (*kainos*) tomb, in which no body had ever been laid. *Kainos* here would have to mean new in kind; certainly an unused tomb could not be merely refurbished.

In fact, the Bible suggests that the old sky and earth will be completely destroyed. Peter says that the present atmosphere will "pass away" (2 Pet. 3:10). Arndt-Gingrich says the verb here means "to come to an end," "disappear."[4] Peter also says that the earth and the works in it "will be burned up," and that "the elements will be dissolved" (vs. 11). Therefore, the new heavens and new earth will no doubt be completely new in kind.

The important thing, of course, is that whatever the composition of our new environment, God is there:

> And I heard a loud voice from the throne saying, "Behold the dwelling of God is with men. He will dwell with them, and they shall be his people, and God himself will be with them; he will wipe away every tear from their eyes, and death shall be no more, neither shall there be mourning nor crying nor pain any more, for the former things have passed away."
>
> Revelation 21:3-4

God is certainly able to design an environment perfectly suited to our needs. And, of course, our greatest need is to be with him.

We Seek the City to Come

The writer to the Hebrews says, "We have here no permanent city, but we seek the city that is coming" *(Heb. 13:14). In that "city" we will find our inheritance waiting, reserved for us by God. Presently we will have to maintain faith, for faith allows God's power to keep us close to him. Then, on that tomorrow which will always be new, we will begin to enjoy our inheritance. This is guaranteed by the presence of the indwelling Spirit (Eph. 1:13-14).

Someone may be tempted to ask: "Are you Christians not mercenary? Always concerned about rewards! Can't you ever serve God just for the sake of serving God?" A just question, but, in the expressive words of C. S. Lewis:

> Heaven offers nothing that a mercenary soul can desire. It is safe to tell the pure in heart that they shall see God, for only the pure in heart want to. There are rewards that do not sully motives . . . . Love, by definition, seeks to enjoy its object.[5]

The heavenly reward is *God!* The inheritance is to know, love, and be with God and Christ. This inheritance could hold no interest for a mercenary person, but it utterly consumes the unselfish. They want to know at long last the God whose love has made their victory possible. That is precisely what is promised in the Christian doctrine of heaven.

[1] Carl F. H. Henry, *Faith at the Frontiers* (Chicago: Moody Press, 1969), p. 66.

[2] Compare the scholarly discussion in E. G. Selwyn's *The First Epistle of St. Peter* (London: Macmillan, 1969), pp. 124–125.

[3] Rupert Brook, *The Great Lover*, lines 56-68.

[4] Arndt-Gingrich, op. cit., p. 631.

[5] C.S. Lewis, *The Problem of Pain* (New York: Macmillan, 1943), p. 145.